TEMPO DI MARCIA

Stories from the history of Central Pennsylvania Youth Ballet

Gotham Books

30 N Gould St.
Ste. 20820, Sheridan, WY 82801
https://gothambooksinc.com/

Phone: 1 (307) 464-7800

© 2024 *Craig Jurgensen, M.D.* All rights reserved.

No part of this book may be reproduced, stored in a retrieval system, or transmitted by any means without the written permission of the author.

Published by Gotham Books (June 18, 2024)

ISBN: 979-8-88775-867-1 (H)
ISBN: 979-8-88775-865-7 (P)
ISBN: 979-8-88775-866-4 (E)

Because of the dynamic nature of the Internet, any web addresses or links contained in this book may have changed since publication and may no longer be valid.

The views expressed in this work are solely those of the author and do not necessarily reflect the views of the publisher, and the publisher hereby disclaims any responsibility for them.

TEMPO DI MARCIA

Stories from the history of Central Pennsylvania Youth Ballet

Marcia at the easel, 1945
Front cover photograph by Rosalie O'Conner

Craig Jurgensen

Contents

Introduction 1
Dedication 4
Personalities
    Barbara Weisberger (In the Beginning).. 7
    Andre de Ribere (Andre "Drosselmeyer")..................................... 14
    Marcia Dale Weary (Tempo di Marcia) 20
    Kenneth Laws (The Laws of Ballet) 28
    Robert Gregor (A Tall Order)... 37
    Richard Cook (The Cook Book) 40
    Darla Hoover (Darla-ing of CPYB 46
    Haydee Greene (Ballet Super Mom)... 52
    Nancie Imler ("And a little child shall lead them") 58
    Betty Smith (Tutu for Teddy)... 64
    Sandra Weary (Behind the Scenes) 73
Timeline – Chronology.. 82
Profiles
    Sampling Of CPYB Students 90
    Staff, Faculty, Administration 100
    Spotlights 112
Professional Dancers 117
Index 118
Acknowledgements 121
Marcia Dale Weary, Obituary 123
Administrative Staff 125

INTRODUCTION

Tempo di Marcia. Note the capital M...for Marcia. The proper name, Marcia, is the person who over 55 years gave her time (tempo) for the Central Pennsylvania Youth Ballet (CPYB). The more familiar term, tempo di marcia, with a small m...for march, is called a tempo marking. It is placed in the top left corner of a sheet of music, and indicates that the work should be performed according to the time marking of a march. As dance is a form of music, it is reasonable to observe that the tempo of the Central Pennsylvania Youth Ballet has been conducted according to its founder, Marcia Dale Weary. CPYB time began when the Marcia Dale School of Dance was formed in 1955. Time continued when the school was incorporated and renamed the Central Pennsylvania Youth Ballet in 1979. Over the years of its existence, students, staff, and administrators have invested their time for learning, teaching, and managing the school according to its director. Whether it be in class or rehearsal, back stage or front stage, cubical or front office, costume closet or dressing room, studio or boardroom, all members of CPYB keep time according to tempo di Marcia.

When I began to research the history of the Central Pennsylvania Youth Ballet, I found that information about its history is mainly stored in the rich memories of its founders. Uncovering much of that historical detail has been for me illuminating and fascinating. To date, the only written historical documents include class lists, curricular outlines, syllabus forms, faculty rosters, and financial reports. But these lack personality and humanity. The human stories of CPYB are vital and need to be documented and shared for posterity.

I found that the origins of CPYB connect in a line to the originator of modern ballet as we know it, George Balanchine, in 1948. Ballet descendants and adherents who connect to Balanchine include Barbara Weisberger and Andre de Ribere, the two participants who collaborated with Marcia Dale Weary to establish a ballet school in Carlisle in 1955. In the sense that students and staff of CPYB since then inherit the teachings and philosophy of the master himself, the line of connection between the 2010 CPYB student of today and

George Balanchine is direct. Students and graduates of CPYB thus represent a long line of cultural influence.

Many of the persons whom I interviewed for this writing project used the phrase "the magic of CPYB" when they were asked what is special about this school. I believe that special magic is the pedagogic inheritance which I have described. The same individuals who carry and promulgate the Balanchine art form of dance have remained involved and influential in this school since its inception and during its fifty-five year time course.

The list of CPYB teachers and mentors over the decades includes numerous individuals who have strong institutional roots. As of the year 2010, they include:

> Barbara Weisberger, age 84, first student in Balanchine's School of American Ballet.
> Andre de Ribere, age 95, friend and confidant of George Balanchine.
> Kenneth Laws, who applied the science of physics to the art of ballet.
> Robert Gregor, age 84, engineer, presided over the ballet Board during its expansion.
> Marcia Dale Weary, age 75, founder of the first ballet school in Carlisle in 1955.
> Betty Smith, who brought professional costume design and production to CPYB.
> Maurinda Wingard, first Executive Director, directed its expansion to professional theater.
> Darla Hoover, of New York City Ballet, brought Balanchine choreography to CPYB.
> Richard Cook, first CPYB resident choreographer, brought original ballets to the school.
> Alan Hineline, combined the roles of choreographer and administrator as CEO in 2009.
> Haydee Greene, sought freedom from Cuba, brought three generations to dance in CPYB.

The history of CPYB is both personal and epical. I am honored and pleased to have spoken with all the individuals named above and to have recorded their interesting and passionate stories. This book tells the interconnected histories of the founders and the makers of the Central Pennsylvania Youth Ballet. Its publication fittingly coincided with the 55th year of the school's existence and Marcia's 75th birthday in 2011.

Martha Graham said "I am a dancer. I believe that we learn by practice. Whether it means to learn to dance by practicing dancing or to learn to live by practicing living - in each it is the performance of a dedicated, precise set of acts, physical or intellectual, from which comes the shape of achievement, a sense of one's being, a satisfaction of spirit. One becomes in some area an athlete of God."

Two years after Martha Graham pronounced her credo for living, Marcia Dale Weary adopted it and institutionalized it by forming the Central Pennsylvania Youth Ballet in 1955.

— Craig Jurgensen

Craig Jurgensen to Marcia—"Happy birthday!" (3/31/2011)

DEDICATION

Maurinda Wingard

*...to have and to hold,
for better or for worse,
to love and to cherish,
in sickness and in health,
until death do us part...*

The religious vows for marriage provide one the spiritual occasion to express and promise love and devotion, to make a pledge to grow together in the institution of marriage, accept and adjust to problems, enjoy the pleasures of success, work with and through illness, and if mortal illness comes—to die for the cause. In a vocational sense, Maurinda was married to CPYB. For her, being the Executive Director of Central Pennsylvania Youth Ballet was much more than a job. She loved CPYB, grew the institution to its sterling preeminence, accepted and adjusted to business pressures, endured malignancy and chemotherapy, and finally worked at home on her computer with CPYB business until the day she died. Her commitment, vision, innovation, advocacy, and fortitude helped position CPYB at the pinnacle of education in the arts and dance in America.

The seeds of dance were planted at age six when Maurinda started classes at CPYB. She progressed artistically through the pre-professional levels. She ultimately danced the solo role of Sugar Plum Fairy in *The Nutcracker* and Queen of the Wilis in the ballet *Giselle* when she was 17 years old. She went on to study dance at the academic level some years later at Skidmore College. She eventually graduated from Dickinson College with a degree in education administration, a degree well suited to manage a dance school.

Maurinda's initial work in an arts institution would be to organize and administer the Carlisle Project Choreographic Workshop, and to secure major funding from the Ford Foundation. She then accepted work at Dickinson College where she managed a workshop in Physics under Professor Ken Laws. In 1997 she was selected to become the Executive Director of Central Pennsylvania Youth Ballet. During her ambitious tenure, she facilitated an institutional collaboration between CPYB and Dickinson College.

Among the many administrative projects to follow were: participation of CPYB at the Regional Ballet Festival; negotiation to expand the physical plant by relocating to and renovating the Dickinson College Warehouse; securing of highly qualified and experienced faculty; contracting with a professional production manager and theater lighting contractor; recruitment of Alan Hineline as Resident Choreographer. Her leadership also lead to the expansion of outreach dance programs for public schools; securing of major funding from philanthropic foundations; the writing of multiple grant applications; and the negotiation with the Whitaker Center for the Arts and Science for CPYB to be designated the Resident Ballet Company. Above all, Maurinda was committed to promoting and advocating for Marcia Dale Weary in her scholastic enterprise and mission of teaching ballet to young students.

Maurinda died on March 29, 2009. The Central Pennsylvania Youth Ballet grew, matured, and professionalized under her tireless and dedicated leadership. The CPYB Boards of Directors over many years were privileged to have worked with her.

The legacy of Maurinda lives on in a scholarship fund established in her name in March 2009 - The New Hope Scholarship.

This book - *Tempo di Marcia* - is dedicated to the memory of Maurinda Wingard.

— Craig Jurgensen

CRAIG JURGENSEN

Marcia and Maurinda in the front office—2006

BARBARA WEISBERGER
In the Beginning

Barbara and Mr. Balanchine at the School of American Ballet.
With permission: Laura Raucher, Archivist, New York City Ballet
(May 2009)

From a historical standpoint, Barbara Weisberger was a student present at the beginning of modern ballet in America in 1948. A disciple of George Balanchine, she followed in the master's footsteps and like him, formed her own ballet school in 1952. Next in order came her own performance company in 1962, the Pennsylvania Ballet. She remained a proponent and a protégée of Balanchine and a living historian of dance in America over 80 plus years of her life. Her preeminence in the field is acknowledged by her recent appointment to the panel of the National Endowment for the Arts and to the Board of Directors of Dance USA. The teaching, choreography, and spirit of

George Balanchine have lived on through Barbara Weisberger, his witness and disciple, into the new millennium.

The Biblical reference to the creation of ballet in America is intentional. Modern ballet was created in Russia and was carried to the United States in the person of Giorgi Balanchivadze. He arrived in New York City and Americanized his name to Balanchine. He also Americanized his teaching methods to utilize the physique and athleticism which he found in dance students of his new country. He formed the School of American Ballet (SAB) in 1934, literally weeks after arriving in New York City. The success of SAB would later spawn numerous other scholastic institutions around the country. Each would continue to promote and reproduce the choreographic output of this iconic figure of American Ballet, with his familiar nickname, "Mr. B." Deified by cultural anthropologists as the founder of modern American ballet, George Balanchine created an art form. He expressed his artistic love for his dancers by choreographically sculpting each one with his hands. He admired and befriended Barbara Weisberger too, for her understanding of and devotion to dance.

Barbara Linshes was born in Brooklyn, New York in 1926. Barbara first entered a dance studio and put her hand on the practice barre in Brooklyn in 1929 when she was only three years old. The barre, in Barbara's life, forms a set of metaphorical bookends. Her first practice barre and her ultimate home base studio were both in Wilkes-Barre, Pennsylvania. Barbara's many accomplishments between her first practice studio and her eventual retirement in Wilkes-Barre included a dance school, a professional dance company, studios, workshops, choreographic projects, seminars, festivals, and conservatory classes all through the middle Eastern part of the United States.

"When I hear music, I dance."

As a small girl, Barbara felt the reflexive urge to move physically when she heard the sound of music. And don't we all, at times, move to the inviting stimulus of a march or a waltz with at least one or both feet. So it's natural to move, swing, jump, or dance to music, as

Barbara did from age three until her senior years. For her, dance was doing what comes naturally.

It was Barbara Weisberger (married name, 1949) who said "when I hear music, I dance." She was immersed in music as a child. Music class in elementary school thrilled her, and she danced spontaneously in her first grade class. She did impromptu dance routines in school during show and tell time. Her mother's best friend was a dancer, and Barbara watched her dance adoringly. She was taken to performances of the New York City Ballet as a child.

Barbara's interest and attraction to dance began very early in life. A local tiny tot dance school in Brooklyn introduced her to the play and fun of dance. Then Marion Harwick took her into the Marionette School of Dance in Brooklyn and discovered Barbara had obvious talent. Over the next few years, Marion took her aspiring student to professional ballet performances in New York and Philadelphia. Barbara also studied in Philadelphia with the renowned Littlefield sisters, Catherine and Dorothy. Catherine Littlefield herself had founded the Philadelphia Ballet Company in 1936. By the tender age of eight, Barbara was ready for her first professional audition.

Picture this: a small girl standing at the practice barre in The School of American Ballet in New York City in front of the master, George Balanchine of the American Ballet Company in 1934. (The New York City Ballet would be named later in 1948). The School of American Ballet had been formed in 1934 with Lincoln Kirstein as its president and director. Barbara did a private audition before Mr. Balanchine and he was definitely impressed. Accepted into the school with pre-professional adult students, she traveled to SAB by subway through Grand Central Station amongst a million other metropolitan commuters on their way to business. With the group of other students in the school, Barbara had her first professional experiences in the theater as a very young woman.

To be educated in the liberal arts though, Barbara had other things to learn. And she knew that a full life in the arts included schooling, practicing, and teaching. She knew that a career on the stage with Mr. Balanchine was attainable and enviable. But Barbara decided to enter the Pennsylvania State University in 1941 and study elementary education. She graduated in 1945 and then obtained her teaching certificate. The Philadelphia public school system would be the site of her first professional teaching job. It was in Philadelphia that she taught grade school and experienced the receptive minds of students in elementary school. But there was no dance.

In 1952 she opened her very own school of ballet in Wilkes Barre, Pennsylvania, near the home of her parents.

The Wilkes-Barre Ballet Theater built its reputation on Barbara's back ground and experience with the New York City Ballet Company. Visiting staff and teachers soon arrived in her school to give master classes, including George Balanchine, himself. Among them too was a young ballet teacher from Carlisle, Pennsylvania, Marcia Dale Weary. Marcia brought some of her own students to Wilkes-Barre to Barbara's classes. A few years later in 1958, Barbara would make the reciprocal trip to Carlisle where she would teach and collaborate with Marcia and the Marcia Dale School of Dance.

Barbara and Marcia would share and grow in methods of teaching, technique, and repertory over many decades. It was not long before the first student forged in the methods of Marcia and Barbara would follow the adventuresome path to the New York City. Lisa de Ribere finished at the Marcia Dale School and went on to audition before Mr. Balanchine. He recognized the technique and artistry of Marcia, and hired Lisa as the first CPYB graduate to join the New York City Ballet Company. Many more graduates would follow the difficult road to professional stardom.

In 1962, Barbara formed the School of the Pennsylvania Ballet in Philadelphia. Mr. Balanchine had himself encouraged and supported her efforts so that ballet instruction and performance would spread beyond its birth place in New York City. Substantial monetary support for the venture came from the Ford Foundation, which aligned itself with the support of arts and cultural institutions in America.

Since beyond many good ballet schools there's a professional dance company, the natural step for Barbara was to form a new professional dance company. Thus the Pennsylvania Ballet was formed in Philadelphia in 1962. Mr. Balanchine had in fact said to her "Barbara, my smart ballerina, you must do it." The Pennsylvania Ballet made its New York City debut in 1967 at the Brooklyn Academy of Music and a year later at the City Center in Manhattan. The latter was the venue at which Mr. Balanchine had premiered his American Ballet in 1936.

A cooperative and didactic relationship continued between Barbara and other professionals. Marcia Dale Weary, of Carlisle, Pennsylvania, would travel to Philadelphia and bring her own students to adsorb and emulate the methods of Barbara and the Pennsylvania Ballet. By this time the bond and respect between Barbara and Marcia had grown to a reverential level, Barbara avowing that she was an "evangelist of Marcia" and vice versa.

For Barbara, dance was more about teaching than performance. Her vision and purpose in the School of the Pennsylvania Ballet was to instruct both technique and artistry. For her, technique without artistry is only mechanical. Artistry is what differentiates a true dancer from an athletic technician. Dance for Barbara is a language which expresses and reveals elements from the heart and the mind of the performer and which stirs similar emotions in the viewer. Barbara recognized the wide scope of ballet in the region and the value and importance of collaboration. To that end she formed the Northeast Regional Ballet Festival in 1988 in Scranton, Pennsylvania. In Barbara's own description of the Festival, she wrote "In it the seeds were planted that changed the face and future of American Ballet. That crucible of talent and commitment was the springboard to enriched dance movement, and would lead to the proliferation of professional companies and to the development of audiences." Many other ballet schools from the region would send students to the Festival to learn and perform. The annual regional ballet experience would continue over many years.

Another innovative project in teaching was launched by Barbara in 1984. With the financial support of the Ford Foundation, a philanthropic friend of the arts, Barbara formed the Carlisle Project. Her purpose was to convene young and experienced choreographers where they would develop and advance in their creativity. Dance students of course would be the instruments of new choreographic projects. Scholarships were available for students in the Project. In its broad curriculum, Barbara provided seminars and workshops in music, listening, phrasing, composition, and criticism. Among the many dancers and ballet staff who attended the Carlisle Project was David Nash. It was David who years later answered a welcome call from the CPYB Executive Director, Maurinda Wingard, to come to Carlisle and be Production Manager. That formative position was born in the Carlisle Project.

Another novel project was to follow. In August 2007, Barbara formed an educational organization called "Beyond Technique." Having already demonstrated that dance is more than technique and that artistry is what transforms thought to physical expression, she formed a workshop where guest faculty would teach the art of ballet. Wide in its scope, classes were provided in ballet repertory, movement, music, history of performance, composition, and film. Distinguished faculty listed on the application of "Beyond Technique" included: Ruth Andrien, Elizabeth Aldrich, Rafael Grigorian, Tamara Hadley, Darla Hoover, Roy Kaiser, William DeGregory, Gennadi Vostrikov, and naturally, Marcia Dale Weary.

Barbara's preeminence in the field of ballet has spanned eight decades. The pedestal on which she stands affords her a good look at the field of dance since the genesis of American ballet in 1934. Her wisdom and drive continue in force into the new century. In 2001 she was appointed as Artistic Advisor to the Peabody Preparatory Institute. She regularly drives from northern Pennsylvania to Baltimore, Maryland, for its meetings where dance curriculum and programming is discussed and formulated. Other honorable awards for Barbara include: honorary doctorate degrees from the colleges of Swarthmore, Temple, Villanova, Kings College, and University of New England. Prestigious awards include: Pennsylvania State University Distinguished Alumna, the Hazlett Award for Excellence in the Arts from the Governor of Pennsylvania, Distinguished Daughter of Pennsylvania, and the Gimbel Philadelphia Award. She holds honorary positions on the boards of the National Endowment of the Arts, Directors of Dance USA, and Research Center for Arts and Culture of Columbia University.

Talk to humble Barbara and she confides that her greatest personal reward comes from evidence that her vision and mission in teaching dance has become widely established. She prides herself that she was one of Marcia Dale Weary's early teachers. Just as Barbara was inspired and instructed by the ballet deity, George Balanchine, she likewise has promoted and stimulated the growth of ballet throughout the Eastern United States. Disciples of hers have gone on to start their own schools and performance companies. Roy Kaiser, for example, since 1994 the Artistic Director of the Pennsylvania Ballet, was initially hired as an apprentice to that same company by Barbara herself in 1979.

TEMPO DI MARCIA

After a recent CPYB performance of Coppelia in April 2009, a reception was provided backstage for CPYB staff, Board members, friends and dancers. Barbara, looking elegant and spry at 84, had been chauffeured to the Whitaker Theater in Harrisburg more than 100 miles from Wilkes Barre. At the post-ballet reception, Barbara and Marcia met on stage, enjoyed some low calorie hors d'oeuvres, and critiqued the ballet. In attendance, I personally spoke to Schuyler, a ten year old level 3 CPYB dance student standing nearby with her parents, and asked if she had ever heard of Barbara Weisberger. She answered "no." When I asked if she had heard of George Balanchine, she reacted confidently "Oh sure, everyone knows him." I then took her by the hand, walked across stage, and introduced her to a living legend, Barbara Weisberger, Mr. Balanchine's first student. Barbara addressed Schuyler warmly, put her arm over her shoulder, and said "learn to dance my dear one; you're going to love it."

Barbara Weisberger and Schuyler Buckler,
CPYB student - 2009

Andre de Ribere
Andre "Drosselmeyer"

Andre with a family of Nutcrackers - 2009

Andre "Drosselmeyer." That's his name, artistically speaking. Andre — the word *en francais* means *man*. And Drosselmeyer is the dramatic role which he played in real life. Andre de Ribere, his given name, was a true creator of things: a family of four sons and a daughter; manufactured tools and electronics; Olympic horses; ballerinas; a ballet school and a performance company; landscape paintings and portraits; and big ideas.

Take a look into history:

The Nutcracker: Act I, the opening party scene. The place: Ecole de Ballet, Paris. The year: 1927. Enter Drosselmeyer, the

Godfather, danced by the boy wonder — Andre de Ribere, age 12. Among the gifts which Drosselmeyer, a toy maker, presents is a miniature nutcracker. One dramatically cantankerous boy in the party scene grabs the nutcracker and smashes it to the floor. Drosselmeyer (Andre) repairs it on the spot, returns it to Clara, the star of the fairy tale, and the party continues. After the party scene is over, Clara sleeps, and dreams of a fairy land where sugar plums, flutes, flowers, and candy canes come to life. The miniature toy nutcracker is transformed into a prince, who then dances with Clara. It's evident (on stage) at least that dreams can come true.

The Nutcracker: Act I, the opening party scene. The place: the Hershey Theater, Hershey Pennsylvania. The year: 1975. Enter Drosselmeyer, the Godfather, danced again by Andre de Ribere, now 60. Dancing the role of the Sugar Plum Fairy is daughter Lisa de Ribere, age 21, professional dancer with the New York City Ballet Company. The Hershey Theater manager had once dashed the hopes of the little Marcia Dale Dance School of presenting its own version of the Nutcracker on the big stage. Andre, now the President and manager of the School, proceeds to fix all the theatric hurdles and roadblocks. The Nutcracker ballet then successfully takes its place on the professional Hershey Theater stage. Marcia's dream is then triumphantly realized.

The stage manager at the Hershey Theater had scoffed at the request that the little troupe of kids from the Marcia Dale School be permitted to perform their *Nutcracker* on the professional stage. He brushed them off as amateurs, and announced that "this is a unionized stage. You need professional dancers in this theater." Andre proceeded to use all his business and administrative experience and made it happen. To fulfill all the Hershey Theater business demands, he paid the required rent, rented stage sets, sold tickets, sought advertising, and hired a professional Sugar Plum Fairy from the New York City Ballet Company who happened to be named Lisa de Ribere. When the curtain went up on *The Nutcracker* on December 28, 1975, Andre himself danced the role of Drosselmeyer, the toy maker and dream maker. In full costume now, including wig, beard, cape, and high button shoes, Andre watches a fairy tale come to reality. He had transformed the little dance school in Carlisle into a professional performance company. The venture paid off too, with a $50,000 profit. Bravo to Andre!

Marcia Dale Weary had formed a new ballet school in Carlisle in 1955, The Weary family had purchased an old barn out in the country, and outfitted it with practice studios and standard dance flooring. It was modest, but quite sufficient for dance classes. But there were no dressing rooms, no sound system, no air conditioning. And there was only one bath room. With the Marcia method, however, of disciplined classes, practice, rehearsal, and more practice, the barn was transformed into a scholastic institution.

After years of growth and development, this small town ballet school in the countryside needed to do big business: to incorporate, professionalize, advertise, recruit, apply for grants, award scholarships, hire faculty, and eventually make its name and fame as one of the preeminent schools of ballet in the United States.

Andre de Ribere was born Norway and moved with his French family "home" to Paris in 1924. He studied mechanical engineering, electronics, manufacturing, business, literature, music, painting, acting, and certainly, dance. The dictionary word *Renaissance* is appropriate for this French homme de bon ton - *un homme veritable de la Renaissance* - a man highly cultured and skilled in many fields of knowledge. A degree in Literature from the Sorbonne was the carte blanche to the world of arts. Feeling a zeal also for politics, he joined the French Resistance in 1942. (His roots for social justice stem from a great grandfather, who joined the French Revolution long ago in 1793.)

Having a grandfather, mother, and brother with the symbolic name of Gene, one could assume that ballet was effectively in his genes. Andre's grandfather was an artist. His mother, Eugenie, painted portraits of dancers. His father was a concert pianist. His sister, a sculptor, rendered the director of the Paris Opera Ballet. His brother, Eugene, studied ballet. The family was a veritable arts bouquet. Thus growing up, Andre had a steady diet of dance class, painting, cello practice, and theater going. Andre was totally imbued with music and dance, and carried it with him aboard the Queen Mary to America in 1948. He tells the story of naively stepping off the boat in New York City, and (tout de suit) looking for the nearest ballet theater. The newspaper carried an ad for the New York Ballet Company, performing that same night at the City Center. Using all of the eleven dollars he had in his pocket, Andre bought a ticket at the box office and enjoyed a ballet directed by a man whom he had met a few years earlier in Paris, George Balanchine. It would be twenty years after their very first meeting in Paris that Mr. Balanchine would hire Lisa de Ribere, Andre's ballerina daughter, into the New York City Ballet Company in 1970.

The mix of study, work, and art has been a healthy diet for Andre over his whole life. Music and dance classes were of equal importance during undergraduate years. No doubt fellow students in the sciences scoffed at his casting as Drosselmeyer in the Nutcracker when he was a mere boy of twelve. The arts would similarly intermix with academic, manufacturing. and administrative positions through his life.

Andre's industrial and inventive prowess in Paris had come to the notice of Robert Hoffman, a leading American businessman and manufacturer, who invited him to come to the United States in 1948. Andre agreed, and traveled to York, Pennsylvania, primarily to start a manufacturing business. His electronic and mechanical patents were of interest and importance to the American defense business. Ballet, however, had by that time taken a center stage position in the de Ribere family. It would subsequently prompt the decision to stay in the United States after the commercial contract had been fulfilled a few years later.

Daughter Lisa, who was born in 1954 in York, needed ballet lessons. She had already shown natural dance ability at home as a child of five. When Andre took her for professional auditions in Philadelphia and New York, he was told that she was a prodigy, and that he should take her initially to the Marcia Dale School of Dance in Carlisle. The reputation of the school had by then been recognized by the directors of the New York City Ballet and the Pennsylvania Ballet Company. That was a good and reliable enough recommendation for Andre to take his daughter Lisa to Carlisle.

So Lisa started classes in the Barn. Not an average Dad who simply transports his child to and from practice, Andre stayed to watch classes and talk to the teacher, Marcia Dale Weary. Then he went to meetings with the Weary family in the kitchen where the school was managed, family style. Soon he formed a management board, with himself as Chairman Andre and the committee of Dad, Mom, Marcia, and Sandra, presided over finances, budgeting, salaries, contracting, hiring, facilities maintenance, and growth and development. And growth happened.

The little family business in "The Barn" became incorporated as a scholastic center for dance in 1976. It was Andre who proposed naming the school The Central Pennsylvania Youth Ballet in order to represent its spread of influence far beyond Carlisle. Board meetings continued in the humble setting of Marcia's kitchen (or living room).

Andre also danced, of course. He did character roles which he was well familiar with, like Drosselmeyer, annually. Over time he also danced in *Coppelia, Giselle, Sleeping Beauty, Graduation Ball, Swan Lake,* and *La Fille Mal Garder.* The audience soon became familiar with him, and eagerly anticipated his dramatic portrayals.

After twenty years of growth, the humble make-do studio on Meetinghouse Road was cramped and crowded. Students had come from all parts of the United States to study ballet in this converted barn. Eventually after years of growth, conditions for study, rehearsal, and storage had become grossly inadequate. An entire warehouse of 74,000 square feet would be needed by the year 1991 to contain the Central Pennsylvania Youth Ballet and its staff, faculty, and equipment.

In his spare time. Andre was manufacturing electronic devices in a factory in York, PA. In his other spare time, he was managing a farm, training Olympic horses, painting portraits, subscribing to the Metropolitan Opera and New York City Ballet seasons, dancing dramatic roles on the stage, piloting a private airplane in order to commute from York to Carlisle, supporting a family, rearing a ballerina daughter, and hobnobbing with George Balanchine, Igor Stravinsky, Lincoln Kirsten, Jerome Robbins, Leonard Bernstein, Peter Martins, and others. His splendid French accent was an audible reminder to many of the authentic source of his passion for the arts.

Over forty years of service to the CPYB, Andre modeled a unique job description. Starting by bringing his young daughter for dance lessons, then joining the school's Board of Directors, then becoming its President, and then dancing character roles on the stage. Andre was truly all things to everyone. Summing it up, Andre was the French connection, the corporate founder, the impresario, the Balanchine contact, the philanthropist, and lobbyist. He was also the strong arm, the mouth piece, the soft heart, the corporate pilot, and the Chairman of the Board.

His style and enthusiasm and effectiveness was echoed by another father of a young dancer, Bob Gregor, who filled the Andre mold, including performing a major dramatic role in the *Nutcracker*. Then another dancer's father, Ken Laws, also filled the Andre mold, including a major character role in the *Nutcracker*. These three gentlemen have been nominated Founding Fathers of CPYB, and have been continuously supportive and essential to the organization for over half a century.

Andre, still active and creative in the arts at age 95, now lives in a comfortable studio apartment (emphasis on *studio*) in York, Pennsylvania. Enter his home for a visit, and you hear the music of Tchaikovsky, Ravel, or Debussy. Andre steps up from his easel where he spends part of every day. Behind him on the wall is a painting of Lisa de Ribere, as a seven year old dancer in a tutu and ballet slippers, painted by Eugenie de Ribere, Andre's mother. We converse with the sound of Tchaikovsky's *Nutcracker Suite* in the background. Andre is gentile and magnificent, and ushers me to the kitchen table where we talk about painting, music, and ballet. With his rich French accent, he pronounces "ballet" properly, *en francais*. On the canvas in his studio is a portrait which he has just completed of the Founding Fathers of the CPYB: Ken Laws, Bob Gregor, and himself. In the portrait, Andre is in the central position, center of the core, the corps de ballet, and the esprit de corps.

He has his ticket for *Coppelia* ballet, to be performed at Whitaker Center for Science and the Arts in Harrisburg, PA on April 4th. He's seen and has danced the role of Doctor Coppelia more than a few times since his first trip to the theater in New York City in 1948.

Marcia Dale Weary
Tempo di Marcia
(a dance in march-like rhythm)

The Italian word *marcia* - in the music dictionary - means to dance, in march tempo. The proper name Marcia - in real life identity - means the person who formed a dance school in Carlisle, Pennsylvania. Marcia Dale Weary was well named.

For Marcia Dale, the daughter and namesake of father Dale Weary, the developmental motor sequence from birth, to crawl, to walk, to run and to dance took only three years. Dale, the father of Marcia, Sandra, and Rosemary, provided everything - a home, protection, a nurturing environment, and fun. He himself had studied music, percussion – and also dance - earlier in the Staunton Military Academy as a curricular choice. Later as a family man, he taught the girls ball room dance for recreation and play. It became a bonding experience for the whole family.

It was little Marcia, though, whose name spelled in Italian (*marcia*) means *to march or move in rhythm*, who was powerfully inspired to dance for real. A literalist would even say that her given name, Marcia Dale, predestined her to take Dale's name and to dance (*marcia* – in Italian) to it. She also took his lessons and musical rhythms to heart and lived her whole life with them.

And rhythm she got! Rhythm is basic in music. George Gershwin said so too in his iconic song "I Got Rhythm" in 1932. ("Who could ask for anything more...") Marcia, age 3, got it for breakfast - with her

Dale Weary, Staunton Military Academy, circa 1931

orange juice and oat meal. Father, himself a drummer in a military band (Staunton Military School) would take her on his lap and teach her percussion. The 'drum' though in this setting was the kitchen table, and the drum sticks were the fork and spoon. Using kitchen utensils for tapping along with Dale's rhythm pattern, Marcia was literally spoon fed her first music lesson. What a percussive (and noisy) way to start the day! It made a big impression though on Marcia (and on the table). So at the tender age of three, Marcia learned and played the basics of rhythm and tempo – everything from 2/4 to 12/8 and in between – at breakfast!

Saturday night dance clubs and parties were common in the big band era of Glenn Miller, Tommy Dorsey, and others. Marcia loved to watch her parents waltz and whirl around the dance floor. She recalls sitting in the balcony with her sisters Sandra and Rosemary, adoring the sight of their parents dancing to the music of Strauss. Music was commonly in the air too at home. The living room was the center for family entertainment and music making. Marcia herself took piano lessons, and would eventually play at small dance practices. The piano music of Chopin too, played on vinyl records, was commonly part of the atmosphere. Dancing was thus a regular and joyful experience for the whole family as they moved from town to city as Dale searched for jobs. And temporary employment was what led the family of five from Carlisle to Boiling Springs; to Newville; then Shippensburg; then Birmingham, Alabama; and Mobil and then back home again finally to Carlisle in 1951. Jobs for Dale, a surveyor, were scarce in the 1930s and '40s. The family unit was strong though, and connected, and harmonious.

Left to right: Rosemary, father Dale, mother Melva, Marcia, Sandra-circa 1945

With dance and music in her system – in her heart, mind, and feet – Marcia started to teach early in life. At age twelve, to be precise! The only credentials she had at that point were dance lessons from her father. The rest was innate – natural musicality and a feel for artistic movement. All it took was some school friends or neighbors, a living room floor, a piano - and voila, there was the first Marcia Dale amateur dance school! Sister Rosemary was helpful also in the little dance school at home. Marcia would assemble a group of kids, teach parts, play the piano accompaniment, count rhythm, and cheer them on. She was a complete staff of one - arranger, improviser, choreographer, set designer, accompanist. She was also the audience and critic. Marcia was a complete school of dance – all by herself by the age twelve!

"While visions of sugar plums danced in her heads..." So goes the Christmas poem by Clement Moore. Marcia as a very little girl had visions of sugar plum fairies dancing in her head, in her heart, and in her dreams. To bring it to tangible life, though, she needed a virtual stage, some dancers, colorful costumes, some music, and a story.

Marcia took matters into own hands – literally – with paper, pencil, crayons, and scissors – and constructed her own dance world. Marcia's paper doll play dancers were make-believe and wonderfully artistic, but still only two dimensional. Dance scenes were fun to construct, and allowed her to transform dream fantasy to paper doll reality. She played for hours with her sisters and girl friends, limited only by her vast imagination. It was later in high school, though, that her art work (drawing, sketching, and painting) developed and showed professional promise.

By the time of high school graduation, at age seventeen, Marcia received the award for Honors in Art. After graduation, father Dale in fact encouraged Marcia to pursue a visual arts career and become a professional artist, but her dreams of performance and dance were all consuming, and needed to be pursued and brought to life. When she later formed a real dance school in 1955, she would continue to draw and also teach art work to her dance students as a way of extending their experience to the realm of visual art.

She would eventually incorporate all these elements – the dream, drawing, coloring, teaching, and personal development – into her first and only published book entitled *Only One Dream at a Time* in 1997. The little girl in the story (Audrey Anna) watches her first *Nutcracker*, vows to become a ballet dancer, and accepts her first free class. Audrey is aided by her mother (a costume seamstress like Marcia's mother, Melva). Audrey struggles to excel, and eight years later dances the role of the Sugar Plum Fairy. In the book, another child in the audience that day watches her own first *Nutcracker*, and then vows to become a dancer herself. She greets Audrey Anna, who tells the aspiring girl, "The secret is to work hard and never give up." Marcia herself knew that secret very well.

And Marcia never gave up. As soon as the Weary family returned home to Carlisle in 1951, it was time for real dance classes. Initially classes were held in the Carlisle Band building on South Street. It was Marcia's dream, however, to own her own dance school and to build an institution.

Marcia traveled to Harrisburg at the Adra Hopper School, to New York City to the Ballet Repertory with the renowned Thalia Mara, to Philadelphia at the Pennsylvania Ballet School with Barbara

Weisberger, to Wilkes Barre with the Ballet Theater School. She attended numerous seminars residencies, workshops, summer schools, and even master classes with George Balanchine, Anthony Tudor, and others. What she learned in technique and artistry from the masters of classic ballet formed the foundation for the Marcia method of teaching. Her very own fundamental methods and principles of ballet would eventually become a standard of dance pedagogy in the United States.

By 1955, Marcia needed a private studio. Father Dale was supportive all along the way, as always. Naturally, a drummer himself, he first suggested the Carlisle Band hall on South Street. That worked for about a year, but the floor was rough, and all the equipment standing around was made of brass and wood and made lots of noise. So Dale said, "let's buy a barn!" Barns are a good place to grow things, to cultivate, and plant seedlings – like little dancers. But the floor was rough, and all the equipment and farm tools standing around were for hay and sheep. So Dale – with the help of all three daughters, skilled friends, a friend named Robert Sipe and other volunteers – renovated the place, and outfitted three practice rooms, each with a real dance floor. He built a space for costume storage in the hay loft, a row of wooden lockers, and oh yes – one bathroom. And NO DRESSING ROOMS. The farm building, though, had the charm and even the color of a little one room (red) school house – which it was. So the family christened the place "The Barn." After decades of turning out professional ballet dancers, it would become a shrine.

Then came the students – many, many more, and hundreds, and hundreds more. Marcia had no physical, ethnic, social, or financial requirements for entering students. No auditions were required. The only requirement was that a child wanted to learn to dance. Students would learn the rest in class, at the barre, twenty hours per week, twelve months per year, year after year. Practice makes perfect definitely applies to ballet.

There was business to do, however. Tuitions were low, but collectively added up. There were utilities to pay. The Barn needed to be heated. The business was managed by Mother Weary in her "office" in the kitchen. Not only did Melva do the family's cooking in the kitchen, but also the bookkeeping, ordering, filing, record keeping, and paying of bills – in the kitchen. It would be many years before this "mom and pop" business ever saw a budget. But that was fine because the little school was all about family.

However, the business got more complicated. Faculty joined, and they expected pay. Theaters and the Carlisle Senior High School auditorium asked for some rent. They began to sell tickets to performances and that produced some income. Grant money and donations began to flow in. So the Dale Weary family started to have business meetings in the kitchen of the farm house. They formed a Board – with Dale the head, mother Melva the seamstress, Marcia Dale the artistic director, and sister Sandy the money counter. A Frenchman named Andre de Ribere, whose daughter, Lisa, had joined the Marcia Dale School of Dance, knew a lot about business (and ballet too) and offered to help in the front office/kitchen.

Andre was an industrialist and had set up a manufacturing business in York, Pennsylvania. He sat in for a while at the family Board meetings in the farm house. Very soon, though, he became the first President of the fledgling company. Another dance student's father, Bob Gregor, a corporate executive of a manufacturing business in Carlisle also joined the Board. Bob Gregor knew all about accounts receivable, audits, foundation grants, payroll taxes, employee benefits, equipment depreciation, workers' compensation, and miscellaneous income – lots of it. The two business executives plus a lawyer or two wrote orders of incorporation in 1976 and applied 501C3 Non-Profit designation to the young dance school, and gave it a brand name: The Central Pennsylvania Youth Ballet, Inc. Marcia Dale and father Dale sat at those meetings and gave approval and thanks to the volunteer corporate executives meeting in their kitchen and living room.

She wouldn't be late for class though, and typically hurried off to the "Barn" where a room full of eager students in leotards and dance slippers awaited the teacher's directions: "Now kids – first position, plie, pas de bourree, 25ouetté, grand jete, and attitude" (an actual dance movement) – lots of it.

Marcia's students learned the fundamentals of ballet very well, and excelled. It wasn't long before Lisa de Ribere, the little girl whose father put CPYB on the world map, was accepted into the New York City Ballet Company in 1962.

Many more CPYB graduates have joined the ranks of professional ballet companies all over the United States and Europe.

In the years since, and around the globe, CPYB graduates have danced in every major capital city of the world – in South America, Asia, and every part of Europe. Theater program booklets, written in many different foreign languages, typically start out with a solo dancer's biography, reading "began ballet lessons in Carlisle Pennsylvania at the CPYB with Marcia Dale Weary."

Some CPYB alumni have made the professional tour of the ballet world and returned home to teach beginning students again. Darla Hoover, of the New York City Ballet Company, closed the pedagogic loop by returning to CPYB in 1991 to become Associate Artistic Director under Marcia, her first teacher. Tina LaBlanc, celebrated principal of the San Francisco Ballet, was heralded in her final stage performance in May 2009. With the adoring audience applauding, she embraced Marcia on stage and acknowledged her as her teacher. Tina would subsequently take the "Marcia" role, becoming the Artistic Director of the San Francisco Ballet School in 2009.

Ask Marcia how she likes teaching ballet after half a century – and she responds "I love to teach. And I'm still learning."

And she loves her students and also teaching young dancers the way a parent loves her children. At an awards ceremony in June 2007, after receiving the Governor Edward Rendell citation for Outstanding Leadership and Service to Youth, Marcia represented her life's work modestly with the four word epigram "I'm just a teacher."

Says Father Dale to grown up Marcia
"You are an artist"

Typical costume illustration, Marcia

KENNETH LAWS
The Laws of Ballet

Published by Oxford University Press, 2008

The three Laws (capital L) of the Central Pennsylvania Youth Ballet were Ken, Virginia, and Kevin - father and daughter and son. Ken Laws, the father, followed no written law (small l) or any common parental practice when he accompanied his five year old daughter, Virginia, into the ballet studio in 1975. He was, after all, a physicist and professor, academically grounded in science. (Title of PhD thesis: "The Solid Voltaic Cell.") What he discovered, though, in the dance school was the science and also the beauty of balletic movement - the outward expression of the body to the inner presence of music that is dance. Son Kevin, age seven, went along for fun and also joined the ballet school to make it a family activity. Priscilla, the wife and mother in the family, besides tending to the home, was also a tenured professor of physics at Dickinson College. As you can understand, family life was all about the joy and value of learning and teaching. Home for the Laws family was a beautiful, rustic country house located in a Mr. Rogers-type neighborhood only two blocks from the Marcia Dale School of Dance.

In essence, without physics and bio-mechanical engineering, ballet would be amorphous. It absolutely wouldn't exist. Nor would crawling or upright walking exist for that matter. Being an upright, ambulatory organism, most of us do everything physical without ever knowing or appreciating the concepts of mass, gravity, balance, force, or torque. Awareness of Newton's first law of motion ("The motion of an object not subjected to external forces continues indefinitely.") does not improve our enjoyment of athletics. And knowing Newton's second law of motion ("Acceleration of an object equals net force divided by its mass.") does not improve our enjoyment of dance. That these two astounding discoveries, however, were written as laws of nature and studied by Professor Laws, requires that we at least accept that without the reality of force and movement upon mass, we would not be able to even sit and read this page of text, much less execute a tour *en l'air,* or *jete en tourant,* or *pirouette.*

But Professor Laws knew all this, and proved it scientifically in the laboratory. And he published his own Newtonian laws of ballet in an article entitled "Kinesiology for Dance" in 1978. Interest and acceptance for physics and ballet among Ken's scientific colleagues, however, in the physics department at Dickinson College was, let's say, hypothermic. One pure scientist intimated that the application of science to dance was "frivolous" and didn't warrant the time of an academic scientist. A newspaper reporter from the Philadelphia Inquirer criticized the "Kinesiology for Dance" article with the comment "Professor Laws wants to reduce ballet to a science." (Ken himself was not sure whether the newspaper critic was demoting ballet alone or all of science in general.) The Marcia Dale Dance studio would nevertheless become Ken's laboratory for scientific observations. Later, the scientific method applied to ballet would move to the physics laboratory at Dickinson College where weights, velocities, angles, and rotational forces were calculated upon student and professional dance subjects.

Dr. Laws published his first book, *The Physics of Dance*, in 1984, followed by a second book in 1994, *Physics, Dance, and the Pas de Deux*. A third book, *Physics and the Art of Dance*, was published in 2002 by Oxford University Press. The Second Edition was published in 2008. If the local institution of higher learning in Carlisle was initially cautious about the concept of physics and art, the broader academic community was fascinated and even ravenous for Ken's discoveries and teachings. Ken answered inquiries from scholars and scientists from New Jersey to California, and provided physics workshops and seminars in colleges and universities around the country and around the world - in Mexico, Italy, Canada, Indonesia, and Argentina. In the year 2002, Ken participated in the International Conference of Physics Education held in India. Ken presented didactic seminars to professional dance companies at the San Francisco Ballet, the New York City Ballet, the American Ballet Theater, the Atlanta Ballet, the Pacific Northwest Ballet, and many others.

Though his published work and research printed the institutional name of the Central Pennsylvania Youth Ballet, his own presentations in collegiate and professional classes around the world represented the fundamental principles of physics and of rigorous research. Back home, however, in The Barn, Marcia Dale Weary herself had developed a purely artistic curriculum and a teaching syllabus which she alone formulated through years of study and experience. The Marcia Method grew and expanded widely and earned its own reputation and influence worldwide. All the while, Ken's scholastic pursuits in the field of "Bodies in Motion" achieved wide recognition and authority in the scientific and the academic arenas.

So how did this revelation in dance happen to a 40-year-old professor of physics? Ken had plenty going on in his professional life and with his scholastic and administrative duties at Dickinson College to keep him busy. The philosopher Carl Jung theorized that a transition may occur in mid life when one identifies novel elements which lead one in a new direction. Jungian philosophy aside, Ken was mainly being a good dad. When his five and seven year old children went to their first class at the Marcia Dale School of Dance in 1975 and said "Please come with us to class, Daddy," he did. Ken put on ballet slippers and a leotard, and standing 6' 2" tall, joined the preteen class of neophytes. Though he was certainly not physically or artistically ready for the main stage six months later, he would voluntarily go back stage and help with equipment and staging. He even became specialized at pulling the curtain to a musical cue. Theater in one sense is all about timing, he had heard.

Then it happened: standing at the curtain pull station back stage, Ken looked over at the lead dance couple preparing for their grand entrance. The couple stood quietly, did some warming exercises, took smooth deep breaths together, gently flexed their limbs, and awaited their cue from the music. Ken was entranced with what was at once a private and privileged look at the culmination of years of instruction, and countless hours of practice as he observed a couple poised to perform before a live audience.

It was a transforming moment for Ken. A psychologist would refer to an epiphany, a moment of sudden intuitive understanding. In his mind, Ken theorized the physical body as both mechanical and artful in the formation of dance. Ken then raised the curtain, and the couple's pas de deux was performed beautifully. The scene finished. Ken realized, though, that he had raised the curtain on his own new career in the arts.

Dance classes for Ken were fun and the beauty of sharing dance with others made very good musical sense to him. His own early musical training had paved the way for collaboration and partnering. His natural piano talent was paired with the complementary talent of a college friend, and the two together made a fine; Jazz combo.

However, starting elementary dance lessons at age forty was a huge challenge. The contrast in age and maturity at the youth ballet school though disappeared when the sharing involved rhythm, harmony, and best of all, learning. The dance couple, or pas de deux, represented for Ken the essence of partnering, each person supporting and revealing the best in each other. The party of two, basically, is the most familiar composition for all dance, whatever its ethnic or cultural form. Eventually the actual science of the pas de deux would become the subject and title of his second published book in 1994, *Physics, Dance, and the Pas de Deux*.

The first public performance for Ken was in 1975 when the Marcia Dale School presented its first *Nutcracker* on the Hershey

Theater stage. Dance enthusiasts in the audience noted how well the father in the opening party scene was dancing the character role.

From the business point of view, though, there had been lots or work and deliberation required for this particular performance in the Hershey Theater. As a good father, Ken had offered to help the school in the Board room. He would start attending Board meetings in the Dale Weary home with Andre de Ribere as Chairman, Dale Weary as father/manager, Melva Weary as seamstress, Sandy Weary as money counter, and Marcia herself. At this point, the ballet school was truly a "mom and pop business," or commercially speaking, a family-run corporation. Ultimately the name of "Central Pennsylvania Youth Ballet" was suggested by Andre de Ribere and adopted. The school was incorporated in 1976 as a non-profit organization.

If acceptance by the academic community at Dickinson College was initially lukewarm, it began to heat up in 1977. It helped too that Ken was Associate Dean of the College as well as Chairman of the Academic Standards Committee. It allowed him to devote and focus a considerable amount of professional and academic time to the Youth Ballet. The academic reputation which Ken had established in the field of science and arts was now widely recognized. And this was fine with Dickinson College.

Ken conceived of the idea of a summer school program for CPYB in 1977. A summer school session for dance could make use of facilities at the College during June and July. This would also be the time to integrate CPYB and the College administratively. Thus Dickinson dormitories, cafeteria, social hall, and theater space were made available for ballet students who would come from all over the United States. Special staff and faculty were hired. With the success of summer school programs over the following years, the College would eventually authorize a dance curriculum and award credit for matriculated students of the College to enroll in ballet classes at CPYB in 1983. And of course since Ken was by then a full professor at the College, he would be qualified to teach ballet too in 1986 (with Marcia's approval of course.) Ten years of dance class and a few scholarly publications was plenty of authority to certify Ken to instruct elementary classes at the Central Pennsylvania Youth Ballet.

With Professor Laws' background and belief in science and art, the CPYB entered into negotiations with the Helen F. Whitaker Foundation in 1907. The newly constructed Helen & Whitaker Center in the capital city of Harrisburg was instituted to promote and display components of the arts and sciences. It selected and designated the Central Pennsylvania Youth Ballet as the resident ballet company for the Whitaker Center CPYB for its part needed a professional stage, and this vente was considered front and center.

The CPYB Board under Ken Laws' presidency considered this to be recognition of the preeminence and professionalism of the ballet school. Ken's professional orientation to science and art became much further solidified when the Whitaker Foundation accepted his suggestion that the center be named "Center for Science and The Arts." Much more recognition of Ken's substantial contribution to the world of science was the involvement of the National Science Foundation with the Whitaker Center. A major financial grant to the Whitaker Center for Science and the Arts funded an on site exhibition of Ken's published scientific work – named "Bodies in Motion-the Physics of Human Movement." The display is to be on permanent exhibition for visitors to discover and observe the interrelationship of physics and dance. Ken's work was thus installed in a museum setting for future generations to appreciate. Visitors to the Whitaker Center since then enjoy scientific exhibits, interactive learning presentations, an IMAX theater, live performance art, visual art displays, and of course live performances of the Central Pennsylvania Youth Ballet.

Another cooperative step between CPYB and Dickinson College came in 1991 when the College offered CPYB use of its on-campus 74,000 sq. ft. warehouse facility for its dance school. The former shoe factory and storage warehouse was then renovated and reconfigured to the needs of a ballet school, CPYB had had previous metamorphic experience converting a sheep barn to a dance studio back in 1955. By 1991, conditions at The Barn were so cramped and impossible that enrollment in the school had become limited. And students wanting to dance were literally standing at the door to join.

Ken's status as Associate Dean of the College and ballet teacher in the dance school made this institutional blend cooperative and natural. The Dickinson Warehouse, with an agreed rental to the Ballet School, thus became CPYB "Home" on the campus. CPYB was thus listed in the catalog of one of the finest liberal arts colleges in the country. Many dreams came true with that marriage - not only Marcia's dream but those of Professor Laws as well.

Meanwhile back on stage, Ken was performing the celebrated role of Mother Ginger in the annual *Nutcracker*. His *Nutcracker* portfolio in fact documents 158 appearances over a 26 year dance career, with 80 of them as the beloved Mother Ginger. His role in the opening scene as (father) Herr Stahlbaum poignantly dramatizes and symbolizes his father role in life. His other father role, pertaining to the institution itself, is as one of the three Founding Fathers of the Central Pennsylvania Youth Ballet.

Back in Carlisle at the rehearsal studios at the Warehouse, he was teaching partnering classes. His thesis that an understanding of the physics of movement would make dance more proficient had become an accepted tenet in professional dance companies. The physics principle of "make the mass of your body close to your vertical axis" would now make artistic sense to professional dancers. As did many other teachings which apply the physics of movement to the art of dance.

What enables dance, and in essence all human movement, is posture. Posture, defined as the physical attitude which shapes the body and all its parts, is mechanized by muscles and is orchestrated by the central nervous system. Applying physics to dance, Professor Laws for example referred to "mass of the body being close to the vertical" to describe the first position of ballet. The balletic result is beautiful stance - with the least distraction of the limbs upon the vertical trunk. Similarly, the grande jete appears to defy the law of gravity - at least momentarily - for the viewing audience.

For Ken himself, though, posture and stance began to deteriorate in 1999. Gradually over the next five years, spinal posture slowly declined to an alarming 80 degree angle. The diagnosis of Parkinson syndrome was made. Medical treatment improved movement to some degree. Further postural decline though was ascribed to an orthopedic deformity of the bony vertebrae. Ken endured valiantly, however, and was able to continue teaching ballet lessons and partnering classes until 2005. Determined to keep physically active, his bicycle was adapted to his postural deformity. The handle bar was raised, the seat was lowered, and a carrying device was added for a pair of crutches.

Not accepting a disabling spinal diagnosis, however, Ken sought neurosurgical treatment. In October 2008, he underwent a spinal reconstructive procedure at the Cleveland Clinic in Cleveland, Ohio. The surgical result was spectacularly successful. Ken returned home from Cleveland Clinic standing erect! (...with "mass of the body close to the vertical axis" - according to the Laws of physics.)

Though his seniority would define his teaching career as completed, he would visit the ballet school on special occasions to observe class and attend meetings. The CPYB Board nominated Ken as Emeritus Director in September 2008. And meritorious he is for his contributions to the field of science and the arts - and to this wonderful institution. The attendance roster for CPYB meetings in 2009 continues to bear the name of Ken Laws. At the Board table he thoughtfully offers artistic, scientific, and at times critical comments and insight.

His personal posture as a father, instructor, performer, writer, and donor to the Central Pennsylvania Youth Ballet is monumental. When he asked recently at a Board meeting how many men at the table were supporting and assisting the ballet school by dancing, only two other gentlemen raised their hands - Andre de Ribere and Bob Gregor.

Ken has literally given himself to the formation, the foundation, and production of the Central Pennsylvania Youth Ballet. Thanks to Ken forever.

CRAIG JURGENSEN

The professors - Priscilla and Kenneth Laws - 2009

ROBERT GREGOR
A Tall Order

Bob Gregor, as Mother Ginger, with eight clowns aboard

Scene: "The Barn" November, 1965: (Marcia to Donna Gregor, age seven) "Donna, your daddy seems nice and tall. Ask him if he would please consider dancing the role of Mother Ginger in the *Nutcracker* next month."

(Donna to her father, John "Bob" Gregor) "Daddy, Marcia said you're tall, so you should dance the Mother Ginger role at the *Nutcracker* at the Carlisle High School."

(Bob wonders aloud) "That's interesting. I am tall. I like the theater. I've done lots of singing in the theater. But I never DANCED. I'm sure I can learn the part. I wonder what sort of fancy costume I'd have to wear. Sounds like it may be fun. Tell Marcia I'll do it."

(Donna answers to Marcia the next day). "Daddy said sure."

Well, Bob got to stand tall alright, about eight feet worth. Mother Ginger, in the final scene of *The Nutcracker*, stands inside her enormous costume on stilts. And the role was easy to learn, just walk on stage and wave to the crowd. As to the special costume, well it was a dress. With special accessories: flowered headdress, gloves to the elbow, a flowery bouquet, and 2" wide lipstick. Mother Ginger smiles ear to ear, waves a lace fan in one hand and blows kisses with the other. For Bob, a corporate executive and mechanical engineer, that was a true role reversal. In his business life, the daily costume was pin stripe suit, neck tie, and cufflinks. This business man knew nothing about cross dressing for the theater. The only legitimate experience he had had in the theater was to sing in a barbershop chorus and choral groups.

But Bob agreed and said to Donna, "tell Marcia I'll do it just once."

That was 1965. Over the next twenty eight seasons (!) of the *Nutcracker*, Bob Gregor would play Mother Ginger with more fun, more flourish, frills, and fanfare with each performance. And more fans too. The audience grew to expect to see Mr. Gregor as Mrs. Ginger every year. When his business relocated to Buffalo in 1988, Bob flew in a private jet to Hershey to play the role the audience had come to expect: Mother Ginger, guardian of eight little clowns hidden beneath his/her 6' wide petticoat.

With the success and acclaim which Bob (Mother Ginger) won onstage, he had found a natural and untapped talent for acting. Or was it dancing? Marcia Dale Weary herself told him that everyone is a dancer on the stage. With that as approval and commission, Bob decided to accept a few other dramatic roles.

Over the subsequent years, Bob would dance the character role in *La Fille Mal Guarde, Graduation Ball,* and *Coppelia*. In a CPYB retrospective recently, Bob related the story of the *Coppelia* performance in 1990. He was on stage and in costume when the audio tape broke. The music stopped. All was silent, except the gasp of the audience. Using all his theatric spontaneity, Bob/Dr. Coppelia took over the stage. He improvised and awed the audience for a few minutes of swing-and sway until the tape was repaired. The music returned, and the scene restarted. Bob confides that "that was my finest hour on stage."

As it turned out also that the character role in general gave Bob tremendous personal fulfillment. He would relish and be enthralled by the joyful response that comes from an approving audience that has been pleased and entertained by his efforts.

"Bob" also stood tall in another way, as Chairman of the Board of Central Pennsylvania Youth Ballet. By 1975, Marcia recognized that his skills of business administration and management were needed in the Board room. And in the Board room it was not always smiles, hand waving, or blowing kisses. There were corporate funding challenges, grants to write, faculty salaries and benefits to negotiate, artistic licenses to obtain, acquisition fees to pay, 501 (C) 3 requirements to follow, complaints to settle, tuitions to collect, scholarships to award, and advertisements to sell. And Marcia Dale Weary to please. There were comparisons in Bob's mind between the business customers he served the manufacturing world and the audience which the ballet school performed to in the theater. Both groups need to be marketed to and pleased with the product and to get their money's worth.

After his retirement from *The Nutcracker* stage in 1993, Bob continued to be an active participant in the administration of the School. He served many terms as President of the Board. He guided the Artistic Director through many difficult and challenging issues. There were many important administrative matters which needed Bob's even temperament, insight, and his sense of what's right, and certainly his skill in balancing an arts agenda with a business mandate.

Bob was the President during part of the time of Maurinda Wingard's terminal illness. He was able to guide the Administration during the transitional period before a replacement could be named. (Alan Hineline became CEO in 2009.)

In May 2009, a portrait was completed of the three Founding Fathers of CPYB - Andre de Ribere, Ken Laws, and Bob Gregor. The three of them collectively founded, funded, guided, and also danced on the stage during many years of CPYB history. No other members of the Board of Directors since then have so personally and bodily dedicated themselves to the organization.

Richard Cook
The Cook Book

Richard Arthur Cook, born in 1951, wrote the COOK Book - biographically - for a life in ballet. The Cook Book of when, where, and how to tells the story of a boy who began life in the arts as a simple stagehand; advanced to set designer; attended college and studied theater arts briefly; started ballet school and learned how to dance; joined a professional ballet company as an apprentice; and soon performed on the live stage. He was next a dance coach and instructor, and then a choreographer. He then rose to the advisory rank of ballet consultant, and then became an artistic director of a ballet school. He ultimately ascended to the academic realm and became a college professor of theater and dance. Through it all, he was a dance historian and an advocate for dance in school and in the community. The Cook Book is a ballet encyclopedia. It covers his path from backstage to front-stage, mechanic to producer, student to professor, listener to lecturer, and from critic to choreographer. Richard's done it all. The Cook Book is his life story.

Chapter One: Back Stage

The stage for Richard Cook was set for the visual arts early in his life. Richard recalled being drawn to the photographic and illustrative art work in the *Saturday Evening Post* and *Life Magazine*. Like other children of the 1950s, he had the seeds of graphic art and illustrative painting planted in his head by the father of American iconography, Norman Rockwell. Rockwell's illustrations have metaphorical significance: faith, family, patriotism, vocation, recreation, and inspiration. They describe and celebrate American culture of that era. The photographs in Life Magazine are dramatic and inspirational. Richard was able to identify with the cultural symbolism of the time, and put himself in the picture.

As the only boy in his high school class who was good at carpentry and mechanics, he worked backstage in the school musicals. His father was skillful in construction and building, and taught his young son. Richard then learned how to build sets, design scenery, arrange lighting, paint backdrops, and direct a crew. He learned firsthand about the importance of the stage crew behind a performance company.

Chapter Two: Performance

It was backstage however during a one-act performance of Coppelia in 1960 that Richard saw the light. He recalls being transfixed by the music, the dancers, the costumes, and the story. Richard realized that it's the ballet dancers themselves who transform the music to human expression and understanding. It's the dancers who represent the story and stir the human emotions in the audience. He realized that to really experience the music personally, he had to perform the music. He had to dance.

So he decided right then, at age 19, to take ballet lessons. He would soon learn, however, that initial dance lessons may be facile for children of 6 and 7 years of age- not so for a fully grown adult.

Richard took ballet courses one at a time. He enrolled in the Joffrey Summer Course with a very helpful scholarship. He then traveled across the Atlantic Ocean to the Netherlands where he studied at the Royal Conservatory of Dance and Music under Richard Gibson. He took an important course of study at the New York City Studio of Stage Design in 1986.

After eight years of course work, seminars, and workshops, he was ready to sign with a real production company. He initially joined the Pennsylvania Ballet as an apprentice in 1983 under the directorship of Barbara Weisberger. The Weisberger connection was ultimately to be of immense personal and institutional importance for Richard.

With broad experience in ballet schools, classes, master classes, seminars, and a real performance company, Richard was ultimately prepared and experienced to teach ballet. Over time, he had begun to witness and to be impressed by student dancers from a small dance school in Central Pennsylvania. Barbara Weisberger herself had formed a collaborative relationship with that school's director, named Marcia Dale Weary. Barbara allowed and encouraged Richard to pursue a teaching position in Carlisle at the Central Pennsylvania Youth Ballet. Initially the summer school of CPYB was in need of faculty and staff. So he was accepted, and joined the summer faculty of CPYB in 1982.

Things went well. Richard was a natural teacher. He understood young children and student dancers. And they loved him. Within a year of his rapid ascent to staff position in CPYB, Marcia Dale Weary and the Board asked Richard to be the Associate Artistic Director. His affinity and fondness for student dancers made this a perfect professional position for him. His relationship to students was magnetic, charismatic, and creative. His knack of making the repetition and rigidity of dance class to be fun drew students to him. He was able to stimulate young beginners and also inspire older students. He would soon recognize the ability to create dance itself - to choreograph.

Chapter Three: A New Nutcracker for CPYB

In 1989 discussions began among the CPYB staff and the Board to revitalize their 16 year old *Nutcracker* (originally by Marius Petipa in 1892). Richard, always aspiring to higher levels of artistry, suggested that the CPYB School learn and perform the masterpiece *Nutcracker* of George Balanchine. Until then the exclusive right of the New York City Ballet Company, its performance was privileged and protected by the Balanchine Trust. Richard's estimation, however, of the skill and proficiency of the CPYB dancers was that they were capable of performing the work. It would take extensive and analytic on-site visits and evaluation by artistic and administrative staff of the Balanchine Trust. There would be many legal and artistic requirements. Major funding was provided by the Pennsylvania Council of the Arts. Finally the requirements were satisfied, and the first ballet school in the country to perform a Balanchine work would be the Central Pennsylvania Youth Ballet. With Richard's inspiration and energetic motivation, the Balanchine chapter in the Cook Book was formulated:

The Nutcracker of George Balanchine, performed by students of CPYB

Recipe - How to put it together in the CPYB Warehouse
Ingredients:
* Central Pennsylvania Youth Ballet, 1991
* CPYB students, corps de ballet
* Contract license signed by the Balanchine Trust, NYC
* Acquisition costs and royalty fees paid by CPYB
* Pennsylvania Council on the Arts funding
* Choreographic documents and notations by Mr. Balanchine
* Business details managed by Nancie Imler, Executive Director
* Repetiture of the New York City Ballet - Victoria Simon
* Sets and backdrops constructed by Miami City Ballet under Carlos Arditti (Act II)
* Act I backdrops from University of Indiana Dance School
* Costumes built by Haydee Morales, Costume Mistress
* Darla Hoover of New York City Ballet to oversee rehearsals

Chief Cook: Richard Cook, Associate Artistic Director, CPYB
Presentation: Prepare and serve with music of Tchaikovsky at Hershey Theater, December 21, 1991

Chapter Four: Choreography

Choreography is a creative art form which transforms sketching into living sculpture. Marcia Dale Weary recognized Richard's ability as a balletic sculptor. She asked him to create a ballet for the Central Pennsylvania Youth Ballet in 1982. Richard traveled by train from Philadelphia to Carlisle for rehearsals. He soon became aware that CPYB was a warm and friendly place. Marcia indicated to him that "Daddy will pick you up at the train station in his green Buick." Dale Weary enjoyed showing Richard around Carlisle beyond the well worn pathway to the Barn. Richard choreographed sections of the *Classical Symphony* of Serge Prokofiev. The *Classical Ballet* (Symphony) was later presented at the Regional Ballet Festival. One of the CPYB dancers in the ballet was Tina LeBlanc, whose pas de deux was recognized as polished and of professional quality. So thanks to Richard, Tina's ballet career was launched and rose like a meteor to the Joffrey Ballet Company and beyond, to the San Francisco Ballet.

The next creative work was the Mendelssohn Octet in 1983. A promising lead dancer in the piece was Heather Jurgensen. On the success and strength of the Mendelssohn Octet, thanks to Richard, Heather herself in started a career in professional ballet that lead to the New York City Ballet and then across the Atlantic Ocean to the Hamburg Ballet in Germany. Many other dancers found their pre-professional identity in Richard's ballet work and continued in their dance careers.

More choreographic output was to follow. The Carlisle Project, conceived of and organized by Barbara Weisberger, was a summer workshop for choreographers and dancers from around the country. Richard was able to create and produce a significant number of pieces in this workshop setting. Based on his success at the Carlisle Project, Richard was to move into a full time position with CPYB as Associate Artistic Director.

Chapter Five: The World of Ballet
Beyond Carlisle

Richard recognized that the student dancers at CPYB were capable of performing at the highest technical level. CPYB had already mastered Act II of Balanchine's *Nutcracker* in 1991. So with the administrative support of Nancie Imler, Executive Director of CPYB, further exploratory discussions took place with the Balanchine Trust. What followed was a long series of Balanchine masterworks which CPYB reproduced authentically, including *La Source, Ramonda Variations, Seranade, Tarentella, Donezetti*, and others. Visiting authoritative performers from the Balanchine Trust, including Victoria Simon, Darla Hoover, and others affirmed and acclaimed that CPYB was completely capable of performing the choreography of the creator of modern ballet.

Chapter Six: Academe

In 1997, Purchase College of the State University of New York needed a teacher to fill a sabbatical position in the Conservatory of

Dance. Richard Cook had completed a ten-year faculty position at CPYB and had become professionally poised to move to the college level. The academic position at Purchase was right at this point in his career and his credentials were extensive and esteemed. Richard was appointed therefore as Assistant Professor - a long way from his start backstage as a teenager. His course listing in the College directory included ballet, ballet theory, partnering, and the specialty of the pas de deux. Richard occasionally returned to the ballet school in Carlisle to confer, counsel, teach summer school classes, and with his charisma, to inspire youth in the arts. He showed students by example that dance is foundational in life and is also recreational and healthy. Richard died too young at age 58 from cancer on July 14, 2009. A remembrance performance and photo display of his enormous career and influence at CPYB was held in May 2010 at the Warehouse in Carlisle.

Richard Cook, 2008

Darla Hoover
Darla-ing of CPYB

"When the swallows
Come back to Capistrano
That's the day
I pray that you'll come back to me."

Leon Rene composed "When the swallows come back to Capistrano" in 1939. The song rose to the top of the Radio Hit Parade, and was performed by Glenn Miller, Guy Lombardo, Fred Waring, Pat Boone, Elvis Presley, and countless others. The song romanticizes the folk legend of a migratory bird which reliably leaves its nest in Argentina and ventures north to a mission church in San Juan Capistrano in California where it obtains refuge, solace and protection.

The Nest

Darla Hoover grew up in CPYB - personally, artistically, and professionally. Her parents took her to The Barn at age six while they attended ballroom classes. They were thinking 'baby sitting' for the little girl while mom and dad learned to dance. As it turned out, however, little Darla got some mighty fine lessons too, in ballet class. And the 'baby sitter' teacher for Darla was Marcia Dale Weary. The ballet lessons took: Darla loved it, and she loved Marcia like a daughter. Ballroom dancing for mom and dad lasted about two years and was purely recreational. For the little girl in child care at Marcia Dale School of Dance, though, ballet became a passion, a profession, a religion, a way of life. A home. A nest. Marcia Dale Weary became Darla's second mother.

"When you whispered
Farewell in Capistrano
T' was the day
The swallow flew out to sea"

Darla progressed through all the CPYB levels - 1A, 1B, and up through 7A and 7B. She performed in the yearly Nutcracker and many other ballet performances. By 1976 she was ready to advance to a pre-professional school. She had Marcia's blessing and recommendation to audition for the School of American Ballet in New York City. Of course she was accepted. There were a few others who had made the brave adventure from the Marcia Dale School in Carlisle to SAB on Broadway in New York City, including Lisa de Ribere, Sean Lavery, and Michael Owen. Darla's parents were accepting and supportive of her move to the big city. Darla herself had matured rapidly, and was an independent, confident 16-year old by then, capable of living in an apartment all by herself in 1979.

One of the many benefits of student life at SAB was the opportunity to experience visiting staff and faculty from the New York City Ballet Company, including the Artistic Director himself, George Balanchine. It was Mr. B. in fact who choreographed a ballet for SAB named Bourgeois Gentilhomme, with Darla in the solo role. It turned out to be an audition, and Mr. Balanchine loved her dancing and her dedication. Soon afterwards, she was invited to join the New York City Ballet as an apprentice. She recalls the surprise, the thrill, the elation, and the sense of arrival when a friend in the company asked, "did you get your pay check yet?" Darla probably thought naively that with so much fun dancing, you didn't need to get paid. Living in New York City, though, with the reality of rent, meals, and pointe shoes, she gratefully accepted her first professional paycheck and made ballet her business. She quickly got into the routine of daily company class. She would over time dance in the corps de ballet at the New York State Theater stage in company with - and in The Company of - many of the greatest names in American ballet: Merrill Ashley, Sean Lavery, Suzanne Farrell, Peter Martins, Kyra Nichols, Jacques d'Amboise Patricia McBride, Helgi Tomasson, Heather Watts, Adam Luders, and others. Ballets in which Darla was the featured soloist included *Rossini Quartets, Sonata di Scarlatti,*

Jerome Robbins's F*anfare, The Nutcracker, La Valse, Chaconne, Ballo della Regina, Harlequinade, Eight Easy Pieces,* and countless others.

Darla retired from New York City Ballet in 1991. She had a new focus by that time - a son named Trevor Felixbrod, born to Darla and her then husband Gary. Trevor, of course, began ballet lessons himself and would progress rapidly, and eventually follow his mother's professional course into the School of American Ballet in 2008. His future in ballet will almost certainly include an audition and career with a professional ballet company.

The legacy of George Balanchine and the repertory of the New York City Ballet Company fortunately instilled itself and became sanctified in Darla, personally and professionally. With her experience over ten years under the direction and tutelage of Mr. B. himself, Darla was the embodiment of the spirit and the ethos of the Balanchine creation. The Balanchine Trust entrusted her with the responsibility of teaching, coaching, and certifying choreographic works of the Master which had been protected by copyright law. Darla traveled world wide on and with the authority of George Balanchine, and served as repetiteur for *The Nutcracker, Raymonda Variations, Serenade, Divertimento #15, Valse Fantaisie, Allegro Brillante, Stars and Stripes, Tarantella,* and others. She also staged works for Peter Martins, including *Eight Easy Pieces and Fearful Symmetries.*

The Ballet Academy East is a vibrant school for dance on Manhattan's Upper East Side, established in 1979 by Julia Dubno. In 1994 BAE was in need of an experienced teacher who could formulate a ballet curriculum for youth and prepare a teaching syllabus. Darla was just what the fifteen-year-old school needed. She joined the staff and was soon promoted to Associate Artistic Director in 1995. Her function as Coordinator of the Graded Level Program places her at the foundational level of young ballet students. Darla estimates that she now divides her professional time between two fundamental and demanding scholastic centers - BAE in New York City for approximately 70% of her time, and CPYB the other 30%. If you count, however, the planning, traveling, and time for creative thinking, it's more like 100% and 100%.

Darla and her life partner, Jonathan Riseling, are a true and complete dance couple. Jonathan himself had danced professionally with Alvin Ailey American Dance Theater and taught at the Jamison

Project, Danspace, and Ballet Academy East. The expression "life is a dance" applies well to them, and their private pas de deux is daily and on-going.

Alan Hineline, an up and coming choreographer, noticed Darla and Jonathan in 1995 and created a ballet which was an effective marital rite: *To The Eternity.* Their personal and professional lives are since then intertwined with Alan's career. Jonathan of course was introduced to the Central Pennsylvania Youth Ballet, where he performs in major character roles and also teaches classes in the Summer Program.

Alan Hineline also came to CPYB, thanks to a Darla Hoover introduction. That association grew enormously. Alan eventually created major choreographic works for CPYB, including *Madeline, Sleeping Beauty, The Legend of Sleepy Hollow, Cinderella,* and others. Their close personal sibling-like friendship has solidified. When Alan became Chief Executive Officer of CPYB in 2009, he and Darla then wonderfully shared the administrative and artistic positions of one of the best youth ballet schools in the United States.

CPYB has from the beginning been all about family: mother and father Weary with Marcia and Sandy; Leslie Hench with son Zachary and daughter Tara; sisters Maurinda and Melinda Jones; Nancie Imler and daughter Carrie; Andre de Ribere with Lisa; Ken Laws with daughter Virginia and son Kevin; Craig Jurgensen with daughter Heather and Susan; Bob Gregor and daughter Donna; Marcia Dale and niece Theresa Crawford and her dancer husband, Tom Gill; Darla Hoover with life partner Jonathan; plus legions of other family connections, contacts, friends, and relationships.

> *"All the bells will ring*
> *The chapel choir will sing*
> *The happiness you'll bring*
> *Will live in my memory"*

In the years following Darla's 1990 retirement from New York City Ballet, she returned frequently to CPYB. The commute from her apartment and small family to Carlisle along Interstate 78 and 81 was arduous, monotonous, exhausting, nocturnal, costly, and solitary. But it was always purposeful, educational, familiar, and fulfilling. She traveled home to the 'nest' at The Barn to teach class, rehearse *The Nutcracker*, stage a ballet, attend meetings, plan repertory, interview faculty, and attend ballets. All the while she would travel far and wide as specialized repetiteur and as the appointed and authorized representative of the Balanchine Trust.

There were initial conversations between Maurinda Wingard, Executive Director of Central Pennsylvania Ballet, and Darla for employment in 1995. Darla had by then been continually associated with CPYB in every way, as student, teacher, advisor, advocate, and confident of Marcia. That translated professionally to the position of Associate Artistic Director. So gradually over the years 1990 to 1998, Darla had accepted and provided educational and administrative functions and responsibilities to the CPYB performance company. Eventually she was elected to the Board of Directors in 2006 under President Bob Gregor, himself a CPYB dancer, supporter, counselor, Mother Ginger, designated Founding Father, Board President, and Emeritus Director.

On a typical day (and night) she would commute along the Interstate highways to the Warehouse for class and rehearsal, then attend a three hour Board meeting, then get back on the Interstate and return home to Manhattan, all in one twenty four hour day. (Remember the story of the swallows of Capistrano - here with a more frequent migration.)

The story of the cliff swallows is real and has taken on historical, mythical and religious significance and relevance. The image of a bird leaving its nest, traveling a difficult distance and regularly, reliably returning home "to Capistrano" for refuge and solace has always had scientific fascination and sentimental appeal. The biologic description of the phenomenon initially appeared in a scientific journal The Overland Monthly in 1915.

When I interviewed Darla for this biography, I inquired about how and when and why she returns to CPYB. She answered "because this is home."

*"When the swallows
Come back to Capistrano
That's the day
You promised to come back to me."
(Leon Rene, song writer)
1939*

Marcia and Darla – 2009

Haydee Greene
Ballet Super Mom

"I've always longed for adventure
To do the things I've never dared
And here I'm facing adventure
Then why am I so scared"

Maria von Trapp, singing "I Have Confidence In Me" from the 1959 Broadway musical Sound of Music

Haydee Lazo, age fifteen, shepherded her two younger siblings (Nena age seven, Reinaldo age eight) from Havana, Cuba to Miami, Florida in 1959. Their parents, economically bound to their Cuban homeland stayed behind in Havana. Among Haydee's vital belongings were legal passports, mother-like devotion to her younger sister and brother, tireless energy, a spirit of adventure, passion for ballet, and a pair of point shoes. She had taken formal ballet lessons from the renowned Alicia Alonso, the ballet teacher and directress appointed by Communist dictator Fidel Castro. It was Castro's plan to revive and to publicize the arts and music in the cultural wasteland that Cuba had become. Art and music and the creative spirit, though, need freedom, and Haydee yearned to express it. So she told her

Remembrance of Haydee Greene's Entrance to the US
Pictured L to R: Rinaldo, Zeny, Nena, Haydee Greene - 1959.

parents that she was leaving home and heading for Florida. Arriving in Miami International Airport, Haydee was confronted by a brusque, anti-Cuban immigration officer who scolded "what are you doin' here kid?" Her quick and confident answer - stated in polished English – was "I can dance."

That was enough. She and her little family trio immersed in metropolitan Miami and America, found an apartment, and 'played house." Haydee made friends with a hotel entertainment agent who arranged an audition at the ritzy Fontainebleau Hotel. Then doors (and stages) started to open. She was soon employed - and dancing before elite and wealthy audiences at Miami's most glamorous ball rooms. Haydee in fact taught some of the glitzy high-stepping ball room dancers themselves a thing or two about classical ballet. She would soon meet up professionally and perform with some of the greatest luminaries and entertainers in the business, including Dean Martin, Frank Sinatra, Arthur Murray, Sammy Davis Jr. and others. She and Sammy Davis formed a mutual admiration society, with Sammy learning some ballet steps from Haydee for his song and dance routine, and Haydee jazzing up her own dance style with some tap lessons from Sammy. Haydee was soon dancing in a number of high class ball rooms and stage venues - and making adequate income for sister Nena and brother Reinaldo. The little apartment for three was their HOME and their American dream come true.

> *"Oh, I must stop these doubts,*
> *If I don't I just know I'll turn back*
> *I must dream of the things I am seeking*
> *I am seeking the courage I lack"*

Haydee would soon meet up with another professional dancer, an American named Robert Greene, from Brooklyn, New York. They dated and they also danced together. They eventually discussed marriage and a move to New York City. In 1962 she moved with her siblings into a modest apartment in Brooklyn. Robert and Haydee would eventually marry in 1964. She continued to successfully audition and sign rewarding contracts in the cast of *Pajama Game, Guys and Dolls,* and other Broadway shows. Haydee had danced all the way from the immigration agent's booth in Miami to the big stage on Broadway in New York City. She had arrived!

Meanwhile, husband Robert Greene had made a decision to become a medical doctor, and had started course work at Cornell University Medical School.

So what sort of work does a ballerina, Broadway dancer, 'mom' to two siblings, and wife of an aspiring medical doctor do when it's time for another profession? "Become a nurse, of course." Haydee had decided that she needed a second profession - one that would provide financially for the Greene family. Her mother-like support and protection to her brother and sister had already defined her as a caring, protecting, nurturing person, so clinical nursing was a natural, and was probably in her DNA. Haydee thus attended nursing school and earned her RN degree. Next step professionally was a Master's Degree in Nursing from New York University. She had two children by that time - sons Steven and David.

With her graduate degree now in hand, a license to practice nursing, and tireless energy, Haydee could accept clinical work at the New York University Hospital. Her assigned duties though were typically the 11 PM to 7 AM shift in the NYU Emergency Room. Here she applied her personal attributes of compassion and human service to patients in a metropolitan general public hospital. She relates that she triaged and treated the whole spectrum of humanity in the throes of distress, disease, and psycho-social dysfunction. And she was good at it. She no doubt learned a lot about people in general.

Robert had graduated from Cornell Medical School with an MD degree. He then entered the US Army in the Medical Corps as a physician. Captain Greene's first big assignment was to the Dunham Army Hospital at the Carlisle Barracks in Carlisle Pennsylvania in 1968.

So the Greene family relocated far from the NYC metropolis to another world. To Newville, Pennsylvania. Culture shock? Yes! The differences in a small town were overwhelming. Among the many cultural and social differences in Newville was the lack of a ballet school!

So Haydee started her own ballet school. She spread the word, and young girls and boys joined up and started to learn the fun of ballet. The word spread, and more boys began to show interest. Haydee then enlisted boy athletes from the basketball and football teams to join her ballet school (!) and taught them balletic moves to enhance their jumping and leaping skills on the playing field. Two more of their children - Marc and daughter Karis-expanded the Greene family to six.

Haydee worked at the Dunham Hospital and other private medical offices. A typical work week would include double nursing shifts plus ballet classes and being a busy mother to four all at once. When the work loads started to pile up, though, Haydee realized she had to ask for assistance. She began to look about for another dance school. She and husband Robert had attended a ballet one evening given by the Marcia Dale School of Dance in the Carlisle High School Auditorium. Haydee recalls being totally impressed with the skill and artistry of the student dancers on the stage. On the way home, she said to Robert, "that's a great school, and I need to speak with Marcia."

Then tragedy struck! Robert was accidently killed in a hunting accident in 1973, Haydee suddenly became mother and father, the sole provider, nurturer, protector, planner, driver, and everyone and everything to her four children. For Haydee, now a widow, there was no time to run a ballet school or teach.

> *"So, let them bring on all their problems*
> *I'll do better than my best*
> *I have confidence they'll put me to the test*
> *But I'll make them see I have confidence in me."*

Haydee called Marcia Dale Weary and offered to send her entire group of dance students to Carlisle, to CPYB. Most of Haydee's students transferred to "The Barn" and continued dance classes under Marcia Dale Weary. The athletic boys went too-and Marcia had an influx of the male dancers she had always wished for. Ballet class for the Greene children also continued, just as mother and father had planned. Marc, David, Steven, and Karis each continued at the Marcia Dale School of Dance.

CRAIG JURGENSEN

> *"Somehow I will impress them*
> *I will be firm but kind*
> *And all those children (Heaven bless them)*
> *They will look up to me"*

Haydee provided by all means necessary for her children to continue with ballet lessons. This included of course transportation, watching class, helping with costumes, supporting back stage, assisting with staging, and countless other ways. She worked entirely as a CPYB volunteer, and used her experience to support and encourage other parents. She conceived of an organization which would involve parents in voluntary supportive and assistive tasks at the school and in the theater. Thus the Parents Guild was formed in 1979 with Haydee's advice and encouragement.

Another project which Haydee envisioned was a Gala fund raising event. She and then Executive Officer, Maurinda Wingard, talked and imagined that an invitational event would generate sponsorship donations, feature fine dining, music and dancing, new choreography, and an auction. This dream was ultimately realized with the First CPYB Gala in October 2009. The venue was provided by ballet parents Lou and Shelly Capozzi in Carlisle. Haydee of course was instrumental in the set up, decorations, seating arrangements, food menu, service personnel, audio installation, clean up, and much more. When asked by a staff person, "why do you do all this work for CPYB" Haydee answered "I do it to make it right for all the dance students."

Haydee's children subsequently had children of their own, and grandmother Haydee readily stepped into place to become ballet mom to three more Greenes - Abigail, Connor, and Kate. They each started into CPYB at the *Mommy and Me* division, with stretching and body awareness exercises. Next was Pre-Ballet 1, with introductory exercises at the barre. Each of the three grandchildren advanced through Primary Division and into Pre-Professional Classes.

Grandmother Haydee is the ultimate ballet mom - a Super Mom - bringing the children to daily class, staying until they've finished class and rehearsals. At home she continues with complete service and custody - guiding, advising, feeding, protecting - just as she has done since she was a teenage 'mother' of two siblings back in 1959. While at the Barn or Warehouse, she is busy watching class, sewing costumes, repairing pointe shoes, helping with hair styling, listening, hugging, and always loving. And on occasion, if need be, Haydee has access to teacher Marcia. Their relationship goes deep.

*"I have confidence in confidence alone
Besides which you see, I have confidence in me."*

From "I Have Confidence In Me" - The Sound of Music,
Richard Rodgers and Oscar Hammerstein– 1959

Haydee and her grandchildren dancers 2009

Nancie Imler
"And a little child shall lead them"
Isaiah 11: verse 6

"Come dance with me, Mother" (Carrie Imler, age six)

The example of a young child leading an adult to greatness has literary expression in the Old Testament of the Holy Bible. The Prophet Isaiah in the year 750 Before the Common Era, wrote poetically about incompatible and unlikely associations and with a prophetic purpose: "The wolf will live with the lamb; the leopard will lie down with the goat; the lion will eat straw like the ox; and a child shall lead a people." The Biblical writings of the Prophet Isaiah sounded contradictory in the pre-civilized times of the eighth century BCE - but strangely salutary. They still do- long into the Common Era. The subsequent Christian interpretation of the words and comparisons of Isaiah attached much more substance and humanity to them. Christian references to the Isaiah prophesy are realistic - and begin with a "Child" at the time of birth.

Modern examples of a young child leading an adult to new beliefs and practices are more difficult to find. Adults grow and develop through experience and education into unique individuals. The youthful characteristics of naivety, humility, and trust, are natural. But some of these modify or transform in adulthood as realities and pressures of commerce and competition make social life more conflicting. Ideally, however, parents would do well to recognize these characteristics in their young children and emulate them in their adult lives.

Four examples of the prophesy "a little child shall lead them" unfold in the annals of Central Pennsylvania Youth Ballet:

Lisa de Ribere at the age of six was brought to Marcia Dale School of Dance by her father, Andre. Following Lisa's lead, Andre, by profession an industrial engineer, started ballet classes; then danced the solo role of Herr Drosselmeyer, then as Board President motivated the writing of Articles of Incorporation of the school. Andre was later designated as a Founding Father of CPYB.

Virginia Laws at the age of five was brought to Marcia Dale School of Dance by her father, Ken. Following Virginia's lead, Ken, an academic physicist, started ballet classes. He later danced the solo role of Mother Ginger and then as Board President forged an institutional relationship with Dickinson College. Ken was also later designated as a Founding Father of CPYB.

Donna Gregor at the age of seven was brought to CPYB by her father, Robert/Bob. Following Donna's lead, Robert, a mechanical engineer, started ballet lessons. He later danced the solo role of Mother Ginger and then as Board President helped negotiate a performance contract with The Whitaker Center for the Arts and Science in Harrisburg. Bob was also later designated as a Founding Father of CPYB.

Carrie Imler was six when she was brought to CPYB by her mother, Nancie. Following Carrie's lead, Nancie, a computer analyst in the Defense Department for logistical support of nuclear submarines, started ballet classes. She later danced a character role in *The Nutcracker*. Then as Executive Director of CPYB, she negotiated a contract with the Balanchine Trust for CPYB to perform Act II of George Balanchine's *The Nutcracker* in 1991 and Act I in 1993.

Eventually Nancie's volunteer activities with CPYB would expand and become more operational. Her educational background with an undergraduate and Master's degree in business education and accounting from Shippensburg University prepared her well for professional work in the front office. Her entrance into the boardroom came when she was asked to take minutes in an official meeting of the Board. Nancie was ultimately nominated for the position of Executive Director in 1989. She left her position as computer analyst in the Trident Submarine project of the Defense Department for this newly formed position at Central Pennsylvania Youth Ballet.

Carrie Imler meanwhile progressed through the CPYB student levels successfully while she finished high school. After completing the summer courses at New York's School of American Ballet and the Pacific Northwest Ballet in Seattle, Carrie was invited into the PNB Company as an apprentice in 1995. Her professional ascent afterwards was steadily up - corps de ballet in 1996, solo contract in

1999, and then to the heights (and spot lights) as Principal in 2002. Mother Nancie made many trips to Seattle to see the Principal dancer who had introduced her to ballet.

Meanwhile back at The Barn in Carlisle, there were many important business and administrative issues and projects to address and solve. Richard Cook, Associate Artistic Director of CPYB, had envisioned performing the Balanchine choreography of *The Nutcracker* with his student company in Carlisle. Permission and license for this from the Balanchine Trust had never been granted to a non-professional performing company, so Nancie and artistic staff undertook negotiations with the Trust in New York. Approval came after conformity with many aesthetic, legal, and administrative requirements. Act II of the copyright-controlled choreography eventually was prepared and performed by this children's ballet school at the Hershey Theater in 1991. It was only two years later in 1993 that the entire Balanchine *Nutcracker*, Act I and Act II, was premiered by CPYB. Their fame and reputation spread across the United States.

Many more arrangements and acquisitions were to be completed, including rehearsing schedules, visits by the Balanchine repetiteur (Darla Hoover), costume building by Haydee Morales of the Miami City Ballet, and rental of staging materials and equipment. Nancie approached and won the support of the Pennsylvania Council on the Arts for financial backing in the acquisition costs. Subsequently there were complicated documents to be processed for license to perform Balanchine's *Seranade, La Source, Ramonda Variations, Tarantella*, and many other choreographic works protected by copyright.

In 1992, Nancie arranged for CPYB to participate in the International Ballet Competition in Jackson, Mississippi upon selection by Regional Dance America. CPYB excelled on stage with its performance of the Balanchine *Ramonda Variations*. So impressed was Bruce Marks, Director of the Boston Ballet, that he invited an interactive exchange for CPYB students with his professional company in Boston.

In 1993, Nancie and CPYB organized and hosted the Northeast Regional Ballet Festival which was held in Hershey, Pennsylvania. The Festival was very successful and brought attention and applause to CPYB and its dancers.

TEMPO DI MARCIA

In 1994, Nancie culminated three years' work by planning the first National Ballet Festival for Regional Dance America, held in Houston Texas. All five Regional Ballets participated - bringing 2000 dancers, their chaperones, and 100 ballet performance companies to the Festival. CPYB had an opportunity to showcase its dancers and new choreographies.

Nancie worked cooperatively and creatively with Richard Cook, Associate Artistic Director of CPYB, and of course with and for Marcia Dale Weary. It was Nancie's job to manage the front office, meet with the Board, seek funding, write grants, meet with parents, plan marketing, prepare budgets, and more. All this allowed Marcia to teach class, plan curriculum, build repertory, and rehearse for performances in the studio.

> *"I tell the truth, unless you change*
> *and become like little children,*
> *you cannot enter the Kingdom of Heaven."*
> (Matthew 18:3, Mark 10:15, Luke 18:17)

The Kingdom of Heaven? What kingdom? (Wonders Nancie to herself.)

What about the here and now?

How about 1984, when you're a working mother and helping to support a family. And commuting from Carlisle Pennsylvania to Washington, DC.

There is a kingdom on Earth: a utopian place where a mother can dance with her daughter to the music of Tchaikovsky; muse with her best friend, Marcia; watch dreams come true with sugar plums, candy canes, and flowers; and then glow emotionally when a toy nutcracker comes to life. A miracle! An ideal world! Yes, a kingdom on Earth! (Answers Nancie to herself.)

For Nancie Imler, a global positioning satellite circling the Earth located for her a little red barn on Meetinghouse Road in the town of Carlisle, Pennsylvania. Her daughter, Carrie, led her there to CPYB by the hand. And she met Marcia Dale Weary, and she took ballet lessons with her daughter.

CPYB is a utopian place where little children start a course in creative movement and music; where character formation is a daily focus; where self-discipline is learned; where athletic activity is done to music; where dance is as vital as school work; where team work is essential; where this wonderful teacher named Marcia teaches you art, coloring, and music and helps you make music with your body. It's a kingdom where creativity, conditioning, self expression, and the beauty of body language are practiced daily by teachers who love you.

By enfolding herself in this dream-come-true atmosphere, and in Marcia's confidence and friendship, Nancie found a real here-and-now kingdom. The sister-like friendship between Marcia and Nancie was personal and sincere. They commonly had creative (and recreational) conversation during noon time walks in the friendly locale around the Barn. During a typical casual one mile walk, the two would confer on projects and confide on problems. In dance terms, think of a pas de deux.

But a kingdom on Earth has to be a business too. There's rent, staff, faculty, salaries, overhead, licensing, and marketing to do. Nancie fortunately had the professional skills to go into the front office and do all that as Executive Director in 1984 and leave the art work to Marcia in the dance studio.

Nancie's tenure as Executive Director of Central Pennsylvania Youth Ballet extended from 1989 until 1997. She returned to Washington, DC in 1997 for a consulting position with the Department of Defense. Carrie Imler by this time was dancing principal roles with the Pacific Northwest Ballet. There were trips to Seattle for Nancie and her husband to see the ballet. Leaving CPYB temporarily, a new era of administration would begin under Maurinda Wingard in 1997.

Nancie's allegiance and attachment to CPYB continued into the new millennium. In December 2009, she was recruited and nominated to the Board of Directors by the new Chief Executive Officer of CPYB, Alan Hineline. Attending her first meeting, she was introduced to the Board as a former ballet mom, student dancer, performer, Executive Director, sponsor, and confident of Marcia. Her credentials for Director on the Board were felt to be exemplary and honorable.

After her first two hour business meeting was completed that December, Nancie left the Board room, walked next door to the ballet studio, sat down next to Marcia who was rehearsing the Party scene in *The Nutcracker*, and whispered "let's watch together."

Nancie and Marcia - 2009

Betty Smith
Tutu for Teddy

Tutu for Teddy - costume by Betty Smith

"Oh thank you, Betty! A teddy bear in a tutu! Amazing! He's so cute! I never saw a teddy bear in a tutu before! How did you ever do it?" said Mayra Worthen, Director of the Mayra Worthen Ballet School, to Betty Smith.

"Well" said Betty to Mayra, *"that's a long story. Way back when I was a little girl, my parents knew how to make things, and I..."*

Parental Patterns

Conn Hargrave, Betty's Smith's father, was a die setter and made patterns for automobiles for American Metal Products in the motor city of Detroit, Michigan. He built patterns which were formed into steel frames, doors, fenders, and hoods; for not only cars, but trucks, tanks, jeeps and war machines. Daughter Betty, born in 1944, heard all about patterns. metal fittings, rivets, assembly lines, and custom made orders as a little girl. And she learned about how to make things - not only car parts, but objects at home in the wood shop using tools, drills, calipers, and tape measures. Betty became skilled in wood working and carpentry and facile with drills, coping saws, planes, and routers. She would eventually apply her craft and wood working skills to pattern work and costume design as an adult in her own specialty shop for dance equipment.

Betty's mother, Sarah Elmore, similarly used patterns - not of metal but paper - to build clothes, dresses, and gowns. Sarah was an artist of multiple methods and media, a master painter, a designer, dress maker and seamstress. Betty and her three siblings thus wore everyday clothes made by an absolute costume artist. Mother would typically cut out novel and interesting design patterns from the daily newspaper, then shop for the right fabric in a store, proceed to the sewing machine, and presto, another fashion creation. This system worked for school clothes, church finery, party dresses, and prom knockouts. Her sister, Sara (spelled differently than her mother) worked in the Detroit Saks Fifth Avenue store and had only to report on a new outfit on a sales mannequin and mom would fabricate it.

Though mother Sarah guarded her sewing artistry and kept her haberdashery skills to herself, the inspiration and motivation for creating with material was absorbed and admired by young Betty. When she was 23 years old, and by then a mother herself, she bought her first sewing machine out of necessity. With her natural talents born of parental genetics, an apprenticeship served at home, a passion for patterns, a clever knack for the plain-to-fancy, and an elastic imagination, Betty didn't need formal lessons in sewing or home economics. She simply bought a sewing machine and independently taught herself how to sew. As an adult the pattern making process and building fervor which she had witnessed and emulated from both of her parents would eventually repeat, with Betty making clothes for six of her own and two adoptive children. That's a lot of clothes. And that's very good home economics.

Betty followed her children into the ballet school and resumed dance lessons, which she had sampled as a young girl. The commute from the family home in Kerrville, Texas, to San Antonio for dance classes at the Mayra Worthen Ballet School was an hour each way, and repeated five days per week. As long as there was ballet class, handmade clothes, costumes, and fitted pointe shoes, the commute was worth all the time and effort. She eventually formed a dance shop which provided dance materials and equipment for the entire school.

Betty provided more than sewing and needlework, though, to the Mayra Worthen Ballet School in San Antonio, Texas. She also taught some classes and worked in the front office as well as the costume shop. She eventually took a leadership position of the school and became its Administrator in 1985.

The Teddy Bear

Betty received a toy teddy bear from her parents at Christmastime in 1949. "Teddy" became her constant soulful companion and accompanied her on long trips and adventures over her entire adult life. As both she and the bear aged, Betty needed to make repairs to his fur, eyes, and nose, and even his innards. Maintenance repairs were easy. She of course had many manual skills that made bear repair a fine fare.

Along the way, Teddy needed friends. In 1982, Betty decided to construct her own teddy bear - and not some simple look-alike, but an authentic replica of the original 1901 model that was identified with President Theodore Roosevelt. Adhering to the original inventor's pattern, she researched materials, design, and assembly for the neck and limbs. She ultimately replicated the true 1901 Teddy Bear with flexible limbs, movable neck, and a lovable face. After the first hand-crafted Betty/Teddy bear was constructed, the decision for mass production was easy. So Betty then began to produce teddy bears of all playful shapes, sizes, and personalities. Many were custom ordered. The newly formed business name of "T. Bear and Friends" was adopted, and was located conveniently at home. The birth concept of each bear was formalized with a birth certificate indicating the date and ownership of each one of the offspring of T. Bear and Friends.

The show stopper bear from the T. Bear and Friends assembly line in 1984 was a special one offered as a personal gift to Mayra, director of the Mayra Worthen Ballet School. To dress her up pretty,

Betty created a ballet tutu, complete with pleats, lace, and fancy bodice. And also pointe shoes. Yes, a ballet-bear. It was a favorite around the dance school.

Costumes by Betty Smith, After Karinska

The dictionary defines replicate as "to duplicate, copy, or reproduce."

Betty Smith's mission as a costume artist is to replicate the costume creations of the most celebrated costume artist of all time, Barbara Karinska, a compatriot and collaborator of George Balanchine.

One literally re-creates art when she reproduces or duplicates another's work. Betty was inspired and skilled, and permitted to replicate the costume creations of Madame Barbara Karinska. With Betty's extensive technical experience, her academic involvement at the United States Institute for Theatre Technology, and specialty courses, she had all the necessary credentials and authority to reproduce original Karinska costumes. In the year 2002, Betty worked tirelessly and completed *The Nutcracker* costumes for the entire Alabama Ballet Company. The audience for the premiere performance in the Birmingham-Jefferson County Convention Center that night in December 2002 viewed a completely replicated representation, identical to the original Balanchine production by the New York City Ballet in 1954. Mr. Balanchine and Mme Karinska, of course, attended the 1954 premiere and viewed approvingly and proudly what would become the *Nutcracker* standard to which all subsequent creations would be compared. Among others would be the Central Pennsylvania Youth Ballet Balanchine/Karinska performance of *The Nutcracker* in 2007.

Betty had good vision. When dancers move choreographically before her on the stage, she accurately sees pleats, seams, buttons, ribbons, sequins, lace, ties, and every detail of costume construction from the inside to the outside. She's able to meticulously study photographs of dancers with a magnifying glass and verify every detail. She can account for every fold, button, zipper, and pleat, for every costume in the warehouse.

And Betty had good hands. The hand work required for the full *Nutcracker* ensemble was laborious, and the hours to complete the task were incalculable. But Betty did it. And more. She would go on to replicate full scale performances for the ballets *Donezetti Variations, Serenade, Tarantella, Tchaikovsky Grand pas,* and *Allegro Brilliante* for the Alabama Ballet during her years of employment as costume director (1992-2007).

Beyond the replication of Madame Karinska costumes, a task worth a career in itself, Betty produced all of the other costumes needed for the Ballet School and the company. That required its own mission statement, known as an employment contract. Every ballet of the Mayra Worthen Ballet School from 1984 until 1991 contained the "made by Betty Smith" label. Her next job, costume director for the Alabama Ballet Company was to produce the patterns and the costumes for a professional performance company during the years 1991-2007.

Show Time

It's ten minutes until curtain time and the usher at Convention Center in Birmingham, Alabama, has just escorted you to your seat in the tenth row. "Thank you," you whisper as he hands you a shiny theater bulletin entitled *The Nutcracker,* December 20, 2002. You settle into your seat. You take a deep breath. The audience is dissonant. The orchestra is sounding tiny snippets from the scrumptious Tchaikovsky feast soon to be served. You exchange a few 'hello' comments to the serious ballet connoisseur sitting nearby, who waits in reverent contemplation for the curtain to rise. You flip through the stiff, glossy booklet and find the program listing for tonight's production of *The Nutcracker.* Your eyes quickly glance over the familiar names, and hesitate briefly on....

Choreography by George BALANCHINE
Music by Peter Ilyich TCHAIKOVSKY
Costume Design: Betty Smith, after KARINSKA

You pause and wonder silently, "Smith? Who's that?" You think, "Smith, the most common name in America. There are probably 25 of them in the theater tonight. It doesn't go with Karinska. And who's this Karinska?"

You hear a tuning note from the oboe. The strings tune in perfect unison. All is quiet in the auditorium. The curtain rises, and the splendid re-creation of the original *Nutcracker* unfolds in a spectacular display of the dreams of three creators - the music of Tchaikovsky, choreography by George Balanchine, and the costumes by Mme Karinska.

It's right to couple the name Karinska with Balanchine. The two collaborated over forty years to originate the performance art which has dominated the world of dance over the past one hundred years. Both were products of early twentieth century Russia in its magnificent expression of theatric romanticism. Both Balanchine and Karinska immigrated to the United States and collaborated in the birth of modern ballet. In the words of dance historians, Barbara Karinska, costumer for the New York City Ballet Company for 43 years, enabled the "choreographic vision of Balanchine to be fulfilled in fabric." Thus stated Allegra Kent in the October 2003 issue of *Dance Magazine* ("Memories of Karinska.") Mr. Balanchine himself was reported to have stated in an interview "there's a Shakespeare for literature and Karinska for costumes." Seventy five of the many Balanchine original choreographic productions were brought to visible life on the stage through the costume artistry of Barbara Karinska.

In the decades of dance that followed the New York City Ballet premieres, only one professional couturier/costumer has exactly replicated and re-created the original Balanchine-Karinska costume patterns for *The Nutcracker*. That is Betty Smith, Costume Manager for the performance by the Alabama Ballet Company which was about to be witnessed on the stage at the Birmingham Convention Center. Hardly anyone attending the performance that night would recognize the importance and the mastery of the name Smith attached to the name Karinska.

Credentials

In Birmingham, Alabama, there were plenty of professional and educational contacts, offers, and demands for Betty's specialty as a costumer. She was invited to serve on the teaching staff of the Alabama School of Fine Arts, the Jillana School, the Alabama Ballet Center for Dance, the Alabama Ballet Gorham's Bluff Summer Residency, and the Dance Council of Alabama. She also taught costuming at Birmingham Southern University and the United States Institute for Theatre Technology. The culmination of her accomplished career in Alabama was her nomination to the Costume Society of America.

Central Pennsylvania Youth Ballet

The original costume director for the Marcia Dale School of Dance was Melva Weary, mother of Marcia Dale. Melva was skillful with her hands and creative and had an inventive approach to making designs. Her costumes were fitting and proper. Of course Melva had many other tasks to do for the fledging school. She also helped with bookkeeping and other business operations. She also made meals, and not only meals for the family but for staff, visitors, and faculty. Melva was the *mother* of the ballet school. As demands for costumes and sets grew, other people volunteered to help, often ballet mothers. Countless parents volunteered their many hands and elbows to the cause of outfitting the ballet students at CPYB.

The need for a full time costume director had become evident by the year 2000. The job description of a person who would design, organize, store, fit and re-fit, clean, and customize costumes for a large ballet school was written by Maurinda Wingard, Executive Director. A search went out all over the United States for CPYB's first professional costumer. Darla Hoover made first contact with Betty in Birmingham when she visited professionally to stage the Balanchine Nutcracker in 2005

Alan Hineline, resident choreographer of the Central Pennsylvania Youth Ballet, visited the Alabama Ballet in 2007 to stage his ballet *Twist*. He spoke during his visit there with Betty Smith about a ballet school in central Pennsylvania where students develop into world class dancers under the incomparable tutelage of Marcia Dale Weary, described by *The New York Times* in 1989 as "one of the country's foremost ballet teachers."

After much negotiation, Betty accepted the offer to move to Carlisle, Pennsylvania in 2007 and become the costume manager. The professional status and reputation CPYB as a production company thereby reached an new peak. CPYB would now be comparable to the The New York City Ballet with its professional and costume staff. Imagine the scale of professional satisfaction to Betty when Maurinda Wingard told Betty that her job and her productivity for CPYB in Carlisle could eventually fill a whole Warehouse.

Betty Smith is a Smith

Betty Smith 2009

The dictionary definition of smith is: *smith*, n. Ger *schmied*, to work with a sharp tool. 1. a person who makes or repairs objects.

Betty Hargrave became a Smith in 1964 when she married Stanley Smith. Betty became a *smith* (costume manager) for the Alabama Ballet in 1991, her first professional company. She became a *smith* to CPYB later when she accepted Maurinda Wingard's invitation to become its first full time costumer in 2007. She knew on arrival that there was a lot of work ahead of her when she saw CPYB's *Nutcracker* for the first time, with costumes by committee. Her personal ambition again was to replicate the entire *Nutcracker* cast in authentic Karinska costumes as she had done successfully for the

Alabama Ballet in 2002. Betty began by completing the Mother Ginger costume for the December 2007 performance. To the audience in the Hershey Theater for that performance, the Mother Ginger costume was excitingly new and spectacular. Very few attendees, though, appreciated the tradition and authenticity of that tall, smiling center of dramatic attention on the stage. Betty knows it will take many more years to complete the entire "costumes by Betty Smith after Karinska" project.

In the meantime, Betty, in her busy little sewing studio in the big CPYB Warehouse, has produced countless costumes bearing her very own label, "Costumes by Betty Smith," for many other ballets, including *Madeline and the Gypsies, Snow White, Peter Pan, Masquerade, Flirtation, Paquitta,* and *Pas de Quarte.*

Betty's approach to a costume plan is typically to first listen to and understand the music which will underscore the ballet. She then watches rehearsals and understands the movement and mobility of the dancers. She then confers with the choreographer and with the Artistic Director about the story and the imagery which the ballet expects to present. Betty then proceeds to select fabric, make patterns, and assemble pieces. Next she fits patterns to student dancers who range in size from three feet to six feet in height. Then she multiplies the outfit for sixteen soldiers, sixteen mice, twelve angels, twelve flowers, eight candy canes, five flutes, four Chinese dancers, three party friends, two for lead couple, and one dandy Drosselmeyer.

And that's not all. With her background in building and construction, and with an army of teddy bears to her credit, Betty is always ready to bring an occasional animal to theatric life. For the 2008 performance of Alan Hineline's *Madeline and the Gypsies*, she built a lion, named Oscar. Oscar was the lovable lion in the Madeline story, and helped win the huge success of the *Madeline* performance in the theater.

"A teddy bear in a tutu," said Mayra. "How did you ever do it?" Betty answered, "Way back when I was a little girl, my parents knew how to make things, and I learned how to design, pattern and then build things with fabric. That's taken me a lifetime."

We're proud to place the label in CPYB costumes,
"Costumes by Betty Smith"

Sandra Weary
Behind the Scenes

Sandra and Marcia - 2009

"Of two sisters, one is a watcher, the other a dancer," wrote Louise Gluck, Pulitzer Prize winner and Chancellor of the Academy of American Poets in her 1990 book of poems, *Ararat*. The 1999 New Yorker's Book Award honors and praises her poetry with the comment: "the poetic words of Louise Gluck create verse which is technically precise, sensitive, insightful, and gripping." Ms. Gluck's poetic description, when applied to the sisters Sandra Lee and Marcia Dale Weary, is more than poetic. It's "technically precise, sensitive, insightful, and gripping." The "watcher" member of the sister duo applies to Sandy, who not only watched, but also played, bonded, assisted, provided, cooked, shopped, managed, budgeted, counseled and consoled, advocated, marketed, watched ballets, and watched more ballets, and loved her sister Marcia, the "dancer..." all behind the scenes...

...behind the table

Sandy is the one on the right in this picture (see page 22) - the one with the sandy blond hair - who is upright, confident, smiling, and standing side-to-shoulder with her sister, Marcia. Her right arm and hand are behind Marcia both physically and figuratively. At home she was the oldest of three girls, born in November, 1934. Rosemary Lyn was the youngest, born in 1937. The family of five was strongly cohesive. The family moved and migrated on multiple occasions so that Dale, the father, could seek and secure basic employment. Father Weary had numerous occupations over the years, including surveyor, insurance salesman, warehouse man, and bookkeeper. Employment opportunities thus made the family pack up and navigate from Carlisle to Newville, then Boiling Springs, Middletown, and Shippensburg, in Pennsylvania. They went south next to Bynum, then Birmingham, Childersburg, and then to Mobile in Alabama. In 1950 the family of five returned to Carlisle, Pennsylvania, where they had started. Dale worked for some more years as a bookkeeper and accountant. Afterwards he did mostly fatherly volunteer work for the Marcia Dale School of Dance.

The Weary family needed a home in Carlisle. Sandy was twenty-three years old and Marcia twenty-one. The two of them had had enough income from entry level employment that they could afford a house for the family of five. They consulted with a real estate agent, Pierson K. Miller. What they requested of Mr. Miller was a house with an attached building which could be converted to a dance studio. (The Marcia Dale Dance School had formed earlier in 1955 and was holding classes in the Carlisle Band building on South Street. The rent was affordable at the Band building, but Marcia wished to own her school.) Marcia said to Mr. Miller, "I want to build a dance school." His response to her was, "we don't have one of those in this little town."

Mr. Miller searched all around Cumberland County, and joyfully announced that what he found on Meetinghouse Road was: "Old

MacMiller found a farm, E-I-E-I-O. And on that farm was" an old rugged red barn, a hog pen, two chicken coops, a two-seater outhouse, a pasture for a yard, and yes a plenty big farmhouse. The barn had been used for sheep and the floors were bad. Mr. Miller gave the two women a purchase price, and they counted their dollars. Marcia said "Mr. Miller, sorry but we're short $500." Being a compassionate man and thinking 'dance school sounds like a good business for Carlisle,' he said "I'll give you the rest, and you can pay me back later, interest free." The deal was a godsend in Marcia's mind, and she and Sandy thus bought the farm in 1957. (The Cumberland County tax designation for the Weary property would change from agri culture to haute culture (word play).

There was plenty of work to do to transform a sheep barn to a dance studio. First things first, work began in the barn at the same time that the family set up housekeeping in the nearby farmhouse. Robert Sipe, father of a young dance student, volunteered to help with construction and undertook the task of installing a first class (for the first dance class) dance floor into what would become Studio A. Other helpers joined the work force, including Marcia herself, Sandy, Rosemary, and Dale Weary. It was a few months before modern plumbing could be placed, with running water. (The previous occupants of the building had not required flush toilets.) When classes did begin in the Barn (that was a barn,) the dance students had to go up to the Weary house to go to the bathroom. That was just fine though with the family since the living room in the house had been used initially for dance class anyway. It was a very homey place. (Ask Leslie Hench about ballet class in a sheep barn. She was the first student in the Marcia Dale School of Dance, and is still active as ballet teacher.)

The kitchen table in the Weary household was the centerpiece for family living, for meals together, cooking, counseling, craft work, homework, and problem solving. It was at the kitchen table that father Dale gave music and rhythm lessons to young Marcia. It was at the kitchen table also that Sandy learned verbal communication and the love of language. Language would be the foundation for her career in teaching, which led her from the kitchen on Meetinghouse Road to all parts of the world. She would meet at the house again some twenty years later in 1982 after retiring from the teaching profession.

...behind the desk

Sandy loved and learned languages. Specializing in Spanish and French, she took the academic route to vocation while Marcia followed her artistic dream. She initially studied French on an immersion basis by studying at the University of Bordeaux in France in 1955-1956. Sandy then obtained a college degree in languages from Alabama College. She then studied at the University of California (Berkeley) in 1962-1963 for a Teacher's Certificate. She returned then to France and took French language courses at the Sorbonne of the University of Paris in 1968. Sandy, the studious sister, then earned a Master's Degree in Education in 1979 from Middlebury College, known for its preeminence in languages. Those credentials definitely qualified Sandy to teach languages in the Boiling Springs public school system, where she began her class room career *behind the desk.* (Note that sister Marcia also had a career in the class, a different sort of class - in the ballet studio.) Sandy's steady employment and its benefits fortunately allowed her to play a helpful and useful role to the family, and to that same sister sitting by her side in the 1945 family photo, Marcia.

Sandy's academic resume, though, took her way beyond the Boiling Springs High School. She desired to teach her specialized subjects in foreign lands, where American citizens were in temporary residence. She had always had an adventuresome interest in exploring and traveling. For her first job overseas, Sandy worked in a US Government office in La Paz, Bolivia from 1960 until 1962. Some years later, she signed a contract with the United States Department of Defense in 1965 to teach languages. (The educational function of the US Defense Department was to offer scholastic support to American government families and their dependents who reside in foreign countries.)

So Sandy went around the world to exotic places to teach. Initially in 1965 she set out on a world wide exploration to accept a teaching assignment in the Philippines from 1965 until 1966; Chitose, Japan from 1966 until 1967; then in Naples, Italy from 1967 until 1970; then in Asmara Ethiopia from 1970 until 1971; then in Kenitra, Morocco from 1971 until 1973 in the NATO school; and finally in Rota, Spain from 1973 until 1982. For those American dependent students living on assignment in far away lands, learning Spanish from Sandy Weary was like being in a homeroom class back home. For the Weary family in Carlisle, Pennsylvania, peripatetic Sandy was a pioneer, teaching in places they had only heard about in reference books. Sandy thus traveled the world alone, and taught languages on four continents: North America, Asia, Africa, and Europe.

By 1982 she was ready to retire from the classroom and from government service, and to return to the Dale Weary homestead and to meet again in the meeting house on Meetinghouse Road in Carlisle. She had, after all, gone 50/50 with Marcia to buy the farm in 1957. So once again, she took her place beside that same sister in the 1945 family picture with whom she has always stood.

...behind the door

The front door to the "office" at Central Pennsylvania Youth Ballet in 1982 was open. The word "office" is used here with your permission- and with no apology. I'm speaking again of the kitchen in the Weary homestead on Meetinghouse Road The center of operations was the kitchen, with its centrally placed kitchen table and five chairs. It was there that the Marcia Dale School of Dance launched its business in 1955.

Mother Melva herself had been all things to everyone during the early years of the ballet school, everything from A to Z- from accounting to zippers. That included bookkeeping, filing, mailing, and in addition sewing, and hemming. The job descriptions of bookkeeper and costume mistress hardly ever coincide. But they did in the Melva Weary case, and also included parenting, cooking, and a myriad of other domestic functions.

When Melva became ill in 1982, Sandy came back from Rona, Spain, to work in the family business. An MDS brand name would have seemed right at least alphabetically: M (mother) for Melva, D (dad) for Dale, and S (sister) for Sandy. The institutional acronym however of much more public importance and broad recognition by the year 1979 was CPYB, Central Pennsylvania Youth Ballet. Sandy was the official first homegrown, homespun, and in-house business manager of CPYB.

By that time, the kitchen office needed to relocate across the Barnyard to an attached building constructed by a friendly neighbor, Wayne Heberlig, in 1985. (Mr. Heberlig is the same one who had also done his neighborly best to construct the charming and chummy knotty pine dance studios B and C in the former sheep barn.) In the cabin-like office unit which he built onto the ol' fashioned Barn were fancy modern day business machines, computers, copiers, and even a secretary. CPYB was by then a 501 (c) 3 Corporation.

When Sandy had returned from the academic world (territorial use of the word) she was used to "gracias amigos and parlez vous francais" but not dollars and cents - nor bookkeeping, ordering, payroll taxes, artist contracts, nor tax exemptions. But she learned quickly, as usual, and Melva and Marcia taught her well. Sandy reconfigured her mind from letters to numbers, from romance languages to finance lingo, from language art to visual art. And the school ran smoothly, Sandy devotedly with her right arm and hand still solidly behind that same sister in the 1945 family photo, Marcia.

In 1984, there was a new venture for Sandy to arrange for CPYB - the Summer Program. Ken Laws had conceived of a summer school for dancers, and had negotiated with Dickinson College to utilize its facilities. The College, after all, had all the necessary equipment - dormitories, dining room, practice rooms, and a small theater. The Warehouse, owned by Dickinson College and rented to CPYB, was also suitable for a large assembly of summer ballet students. Ken Laws had himself formulated the program, launched a national marketing plan, advertised, written curriculum, and obtained staff. It was Sandy, though, who dutifully ran the business and collected tuitions, hired dorm staff, assigned rooms, paid faculty, and more. The summer program roster grew each year. The revenue grew too. The reputation grew. An increasing number of students came for the Summer Program from all over the United States, Canada, and Mexico. Many students were motivated to enroll in the year-long dance curriculum and to relocate to Carlisle. Real estate agents in the region were enthused that there were new cultural and artistic reasons for families to move to Carlisle.

As the business demands increased, a fully trained administrative director became a necessity. Maurinda Wingard had initially worked for Professor Kenneth Laws as Project Manager in the Physics Department at Dickinson College. That put her in position to accept the nomination of the ballet Board to become Executive Director of CPYB in 1997. Sandy then worked side by side with Maurinda for many different projects and assignments. She eventually retired completely from the front office in 2001. The business office by then had expanded even further, with placement of a large trailer module adjacent to the Barn in 1990, thanks to a wonderful donation by Don Mowery, President of R.S. Mowery & Sons, Contractors.

Sandy continued, naturally, to support Marcia at home domestically and personally. The CPYB Board made a resolution at her retirement that Sandy would have an honorary ticket to a front row seat at every ballet in the future, ad infinitum. (The *ad infinitum* means that Sandy will be there in the audience at the ballet in spirit.) The Board recognized that Sandy had put in countless hours of dedicated work for the organization, for which she had been partially paid. It's hard from a value standpoint to pay someone adequately when their work has been sisterly and 'round the clock.

...behind the curtain

Behind the curtain is any place where the audience cannot see or notice. Nor is there ever any applause for someone *behind the curtain*. But that's where Sandy has been clearly (un)noticed. At home she was the helper and enabler. In the years of physical decline of mother and father Weary, and after Dale's death in 1992, Sandy was the principal housekeeper and the homemaker. This included shopping and meal preparation. And there were always ballet visitors at home, visitors for faculty meetings, planning sessions, Board meetings, and even some students on break from class.

The general atmosphere on the Weary campus and its Barn headquarters (don't confuse it with a place where you do barn dance) was to provide children with dance skills and also life skills in an enjoyable setting. Sandy played an essential part in providing within the nearby household. The back yard was open for play during breaks from class. A swimming pool was installed in 1980 for students to have a cool break from classes in July. It had been Marcia's primary purpose to provide not only formal arts instruction, and character building, but also friendly recreation to children.

Another scene *behind the curtain* is at home in the basement. Sandy has been the self appointed collector and curator of theater books, brochures, news reports, photographs, and posters. The foundation basement room at home on Meetinghouse Road in Carlisle is an archival temple for a 55 year career in the arts, all stored lovingly in boxes, files, and albums. And Sandy knows where every article of every scrapbook is boxed, filed, or fitted. In researching this book, I had inquired whether her index system was possibly alphabetical, or color coded, or Dewey Decimal, alpha numeric, digital, or digi-anything, and she indicated that "it's all in my head, and it's fine." Sandy is the true treasurer of this treasure trove - and has so far declined to relocate the records elsewhere in some sectarian institution. So there it stays, guarded and gloated over by Sandy. As long as the collection is active and on-going, there cannot be a more dedicated CPYB archivist than Sandy Weary. (Pardon the pun) She will not waffle, waver, nor weary of the weighty wealth of records.

...behind the table

That's the same table we spoke about earlier, in the kitchen. Sandy saw the need to prepare lunch for the staff and faculty on weekend days. The teachers were, after all, working on the weekends, which most other hourly employees think of as free time. But ballet is a seven day process and dancers and staff need sustenance. So Sandy started to prepare lunch for the teachers. This eventually became routine and congenial over the many years. Thus the lunch-at-the-house offering has lasted so far more than fifteen years, when faculty take a Saturday noon break for a meal and discussion. Thanks to Sandy.

One *behind the scenes* category where Sandy did not take her useful place was *behind the wheel*. Dale Weary himself had always been the chief driver and transporter for the family. His green Buick was legendary. He not only took the four women (Melva, Sandy, Marcia, Rosemary) shopping, but also transported guest faculty from the train station, and some Board people to meetings. When Dale became ill in 1985, it was 50-year-old Marcia herself who stepped forward to become the family chauffeur. (Sandy had plenty to do inside, remember.) Thus Sandy never went *behind the wheel* of an automobile to drive. Now that's a distinction in the modern era!

The familiar quotation "a sister is a forever friend" by an unknown writer applies most certainly and continually to the sisterhood of Sandra Lee and Marcia Dale Weary. Behind all the public recognition and celebrity of sister Marcia is the supportive, nurturing presence of Sandy - *Behind the Scenes*.

Timeline – Chronology

May 28, 1956:
    The first ballet performed by the Marcia Dale School of Dance was titled *A Visit to New Orleans in Mardi Gras Season*. It was performed in the Carlisle High School Auditorium.

June 1957:
    Dale Weary purchased farm on Meeting House Road in Carlisle; transformed the barn to "The Barn" for Marcia Dale School of Dance.

December 29, 1969:
    Nutcracker ballet performed at Carlisle Senior High School; Choreography by Alexi Ramov.

January 1975:
    Central Pennsylvania Youth Ballet Incorporated as a non-profit organization; first President was Andre de Ribere.

December 20, 1975:
    First *Nutcracker* performed at Hershey Theater: Choreography Pat Sorell, Costumes Melva Weary, Sugar Plum Fairy Lisa de Ribere, Drosselmeyer Andre de Ribere.

January 1982:
    Richard Cook appointed as Associate Artistic Director.

June 1984:
    Barbara Weisberger formed the Carlisle Project, a workshop for exhibiting new choreographers from across the country.

TEMPO DI MARCIA

January 1985-95:
License granted by the Balanchine Trust for CPYB to perform *Concerto Barocco, Raymonda Variations, La Source, Valse Fantaise, Divertimento No. 15, Harlequinade Pas de Deux, The Nutcracker, Seranade, Donizetti, Tarantella, Walpurgisnacht.*

January 1989:
Nancie Imler selected as Executive Director of CPYB.

January 1990:
CPYB acquires its first Antony Tudor ballet - *Soiree Musicale.*

June 29, 1990:
CPYB represented the Northeast Region of the United States at the USA International Ballet Competition.

February 29, 1992:
The Mighty Casey ballet choreographed for CPYB by alumna Lisa de Ribere; guest narrator Tug McGraw.

June 1992:
CPYB performs *Ramonda Variations* at International Ballet Festival in Jackson, Mississippi.

June 1994:
CPYB, under Nancie Imler Executive Director, hosts the National Ballet Festival in Houston, Texas, attended by 100 ballet schools. CPYB receives rave reviews from Bruce Marks of Boston Ballet, and national fame for its performance of *Raymonda Var.*

June, 1995:
20th Anniversary of Incorporation of CPYB performance, ('75-'95) at the Hershey Theater.

January 1996:
The Carlisle Project disbands.

March 11, 1997:
New York Times lauds CPYB performance in youth showcase at the Spring Festival at Hunter College, Danny Kaye Theater.

May 1997:
Director of the School. Maurinda Wingard, former CPYB dance student, appointed Executive Director.

June 1997:

350 students enroll in the Summer Program, including children from US, Puerto Rico, Brazil, and Belgium.

June 1997:

CPYB sent 30 dancers to the Regional Dance Festival of America in Houston, Texas.

August 1997:

CPYB travels to Tokyo for its first international performance in the Aoyama Ballet Festival.

October 1997:

CPYB budget doubles over the past 5 years to $2,771,750.

October 1997:

CPYB collaborated with Eaken Trio in showcase performance at Dickinson College.

December 1997:

Darla Hoover appointed Assistant Artistic Director.

January 1998:

Teaching faculty increased over 65%, administrative staff increased 60% over ten years.

January 1998:

CPYB performs for First Night Carlisle as part of New Years Eve celebration.

January 1998:

Alan Hineline was appointed Resident Choreographer of CPYB.

April 1998:

CPYB presented benefit ballet at Founders Hall at Milton Hershey School, Hershey, PA.

June 1998:

Ashley Bouder won first place prize in Regional Dance America competition; accepts an award of $500.00.

June 1998:

Mission statement adopted: CPYB is a non-profit corporation committed to training students in the art of classical ballet to the highest standards, the performance of ballet as a component of student education, and the promotion of interest in the art form as a contribution to the cultural life of the extended community.

June 1998:

Pennsylvania Council on the Arts increased funding to CPYB.

June 1998:
CPYB began Choreographic Workshop in Carlisle.
June 1998:
New York Times described Marcia Dale Weary as "one of the country's foremost ballet teachers."
September 1998:
CPYB course listed in Dickinson College catalog; first college students take classes at Youth Ballet School.
November 1999:
CPYB launched its first website - www.cpyb.org.
December 1999:
First CPYB *Nutcracker* performed with the Harrisburg Symphony Orchestra.
December 1999:
CPYB selected to be Resident Ballet Company at the Helen A. Whitaker Center for Science and the Arts.
December 1999:
Alan Hineline received Choo-San Goh Award for Choreography.
January 2000:
Abi Stafford, CPYB alum, danced the lead role in Balanchine's *Valse Fantasie* with the New York City Ballet; *New York Times* reported her "astonishingly authoritative."
April 2000:
CPYB performed the Magic Flute Ballet in the Whitaker Center.
May 2000:
CPYB opened ballet Center and studio complex in the renovated 14,000 sq. ft. Kinney Shoe warehouse.
June 2000:
Sherry Moray choreographed *Once Upon a Dream* for CPYB, to be premiered at Whitaker Center.
July 2000:
Abi Stafford, of New York City Ballet, performed in CPYB Gala at Whitaker Center in Harrisburg, PA.
July 2000:
Marcia Dale Weary Endowment Fund initiated with $10,000 donation.

January 2001:
: Choreoplan 2001 was announced as choreographic workshop.

January 2001:
: CPYB performed debut ballet at the Whitaker Center for Science and the Arts.

December 2001:
: CPYB opens dance studio in Strawberry Square building, Harrisburg, Pennsylvania.

January 2002:
: CPYB receives $5000.00 from Keystone Financial for scholarship funding.

January 2002:
: CPYB offered Discover Dance program, approved under Pennsylvania Educational Program.

March 2002:
: CPYB premiered *The Legend of Sleepy Hollow*, choreographed by Alan Hineline.

June 2002:
: Jason Reed, CPYB alum, choreographed his first dance, "*Jive, Point, and Swing,*" performed at Whitaker Center.

January 2003:
: First grant from National Endowment for the Arts awarded to CPYB.

January 2003:
: CPYB begins Discover Dance Program.

May 2003:
: CPYB hosted Regional Dance America Festival; fifteen dance schools attend and participate.

November 2003:
: Maurinda Wingard invited David Nash of the Pittsburgh Ballet Theater to stage CPYB *Nutcracker*.

January 2004:
: *New York Times* reported: "Marcia Dale Weary produces students who have the whole package - technical development and a broad socialization into the arts. It seems that ballet companies world wide will be stocked with her dancers" (Kristen Lewis).

January 2004:
Maurinda offers David Nash contract to be Production Manager for the entire CPYB season.

January 2005:
CPYB CELEBRATED ITS 50TH ANNIVERSARY!

January 2005:
Alan Hineline restaged the classic *Sleeping Beauty Ballet, and Cinderella.*

July 2, 2005:
Stars of CPYB Gala, featuring professional CPYB graduates; First ever CPYB REUNION: "Shaping lives through Dance," Whitaker.

March 2007:
CPYB returned to the York Strand Capitol Theater after a ten year lapse.

August 2008:
CPYB announced collaboration with the Pennsylvania Ballet Company of Philadelphia.

December 2008:
Andre de Ribere, Bob Gregor, and Ken Laws are appointed Emeritus Directors on the Board of CPYB.

March 2009:
Barbara Weisberger is nominated as Honorary Member of the CPYB Board of Directors.

March 29, 2009:
Maurinda Wingard, Exec. Director of CPYB since 1997, died at age 51. She strenuously advanced the business, artistic, and corporate function and mission of CPYB.

April 2, 2009:
Marcia Dale Weary honored as Pennsylvania Society Distinguished Citizen of the Commonwealth. Award given by the President of the Society, Leroy Zimmerman.

April 15, 2009:
Bryan Matluk was appointed acting Executive Director of CPYB.

May 1, 2009:

Pennsylvania Legislature voted (SB 850) to eliminate funding to arts organizations through the Pennsylvania Council on the Arts, effectively removing an annual $50,000 grant to CPYB.

June 1, 2009:

Bryan Matluk was accepted into the prestigious Kaiser Fellowship at the Kennedy Center for the Performing Arts, Washington D.C. for a year of study in Arts Administration.

July 30, 2009:

Alan Hineline was selected by the CPYB Board as Chief Executive Officer.

August 9-14, 2009:

Teachers' Workshop, hosted by CPYB, held at Dickinson College.

November 30, 2009:

Bonnie Schulte announced as Director of Strategic Marketing and Communication.

May 23, 2010:

Dickinson College presented an Honorary Doctorate Degree in Performance Arts to Marcia Dale Weary at its May 2010 commencement exercises.

February 2019:

Jonathan Stafford named Artistic Director of New York City Ballet Company and the School of American Ballet.

March 4, 2019:

Marcia Dale Weary died.

Citation presented by Sarah Skaggs, Director of Dance and Assistant Professor of Dance Studies, Dickinson College:

"Precision, rigor, discipline, and focus are all words we typically associate with ballet training. With a Zen-like approach, Marcia breaks down each step into its infinitesimal components. Marcia is a sculptor of the living body. She shapes the body through precise articulations. Her students endlessly repeat the constituent components of a step-piece by piece - until each part of the whole is perfected. Only then does a student advance to the next level.

Marcia's teaching methods have paid off. Her students are some of the most refined, precise, and articulate dancers in the field. She has produced many world-famous stars of ballet, who dance with such companies as the New York City Ballet, San Francisco Ballet, American Ballet Theater – to mention a few.

For her unparalleled artistic vision, her unwavering dedication, and the significant public service she has yielded to the Carlisle community and dance world at large, we honor Marcia Dale Weary here today.

Mr. President, it is my honor and pleasure to present to you Marcia Dale Weary for the Honorary Degree of Doctor of Performing Arts."

"I William G. Durden, President of Dickinson College, upon the recommendation of the Faculty to the Board of Trustees, and by its mandamus, do confer upon you the Degree of Doctor of Performing Arts, honoris causa, with all the rights, privileges, and distinction thereunto appertaining, in token of which I present you with this diploma and cause you to be invested with the hood of Dickinson College appropriate to the degree."

— William G. Durden, President

PROFILES
SAMPLING OF CPYB STUDENTS

Aldrich, Daniela
Daniela studied ballet at CPYB for six years. She has performed in Nutcracker, *Legend of Sleepy Hollow, Madeline, Pandora's Box,* and *June Show.* She is involved with Academically Challenging Topics (ACT) and is a distinguished honor student. She is the daughter of Asuncion Arnedo and Mark Aldrich.

Anacan, Antonio
Antonio began studying at CPYB in 2008. Age 23, he enjoys photography. He trained previously at San Francisco Ballet School. His parents - Antonio & Carolyn.

Anacan, Angelito
Angelito has been studying ballet with CPYB for 2 years. He trained previously at Pacific Ballet Academy and Hawaii State Ballet. CPYB roles include: *The Nutcracker, Peter Pan, June Series, Madeline and the Gypsies.* His parents are Antonio and Carolyn Anacan.

Arbaczewski, Robbie-Jean Arbott
Robbie-Jean studied at CPYB for nine years. She performed in the *Nutcracker* as Sugar Plum Fairy, Dew Drop Fairy, and Snow. She also performed in *Who Cares?, La Source, Coppelia, Serenade,* and *From A to M.* She joined the Pacific Northwest Ballet in 2007. She is the daughter of Robert and Jean Arbott.

Atwood, EmmaRose
EmmaRose has been a student at CPYB for 8 years. She has had performance roles in *Peter Pan, June Series, The Nutcracker, Coppelia, Snow White, Cinderella, Legend of Sleepy Hollow, Madeline.* She is the daughter of Ruth Atwood and Kathryn Shatzer.

Avery, Cleopatra Anna
Cleopatra Anna studied at CPYB for 11 years. She danced in the *Nutcracker* as Flower, Hot Chocolate, and Snowflake. Previous performances include *Stars and Stripes, Rococo Variations, La Bayadere, Baroque, Coppelia, La Source, Serenade, Raymonda*

Variations, Legend of Sleepy Hollow, and *Sleeping Beauty.* Her parents are Vikki and Scott Avery.

Avery, Euphrosyne Maria

Euphrosyne studied at CPYB for 11 years. She danced in *Nutcracker* as Dewdrop, Flower, Snowflake and Principal Marzipan. She performed in other productions including *Cinderella, Stars and Stripes, Rococo Variations, La Bayadere, Coppelia, Who Cares?, Serenade,* and *Sleeping Beauty.* She is the daughter of Vikki and Scott Avery.

Barnes, Edward

Edward has studied with CPYB for two years. He is a recipient of the JEF Male Dancer Scholarship. He danced Cavalier and lead Spanish in *Nutcracker.* He also danced in *Legend of Sleepy Hollow, Cinderella, Pandora's Box,* and the *June Show.* He was an honor student at Carlisle High School. His parents are Clifford and Pamela Barnes.

Cirio, Jeffrey

Jeffrey started ballet lessons at age 9 with CPYB. As a student, he has performed roles as Prince, Soldier Doll, Chinese Tea, and Candy Cane in the *Nutcracker*. He has also performed in *Legend of Sleepy Hollow, Coppelia,* and *Sneaky Pete.* Jeffrey has received scholarships to study at Stuttgart Ballet, JKO School in NYC, and Boston Ballet School. His awards include gold medal at Youth American Grand Prix 2006, Best Male Dancer at the American Ballet Competition. He performed at the Life chance Gala in Columbia, South Carolina in 2007.

Darhower, Marcia

Marcia began her ballet training in Carlisle at CPYB at age 14. After two years, she was offered a scholarship at the Pennsylvania Ballet School by Barbara Weisberger. At age 17, she joined the Pennsylvania Ballet Company. As a principal dancer, she won acclaim, and danced feature roles as Recital for Cello, In Retrospect, and Eight Movements in Ragtime.

Davis, Dillon

Dillon began to study ballet at age 10. He then moved to Chattanooga, TN and studied under Frank Hay and Jennifer Sproul. At age 18 he accepted an apprenticeship at Alabama Ballet. Dillon has performed in *Cinderella, Madeline, June Show,* and *Nutcracker* (Father, Mother Ginger)

DeAngelo, Abby Jayne

Abby Jayne has been a student at CPYB for 6 years. She also enjoys playing piano and reading. Abby Jayne has had performance roles in: *Peter Pan, June Series, Coppelia, The Nutcracker, Cinderella, Madeline, Sleeping Beauty,* and *Pandora's Box.* Abby Jayne is the daughter of Cory and Emily DeAngelo. Her dance is in thanks to God and in His honor.

de Ribere, Lisa

Lisa started ballet lessons at age 7 in the Marcia Dale School of Dance. She then studied at the Pennsylvania Ballet School. She then received a Ford Foundation Scholarship to study at the School of American Ballet. At age 15 she was asked by George Balanchine to join the New York City Ballet (1970). Solo roles included Allegro Brilliante, Donizetti Variations, Don Quixote, and Brahms-Schoenberg Quartet. She later created choreographic works: *The Seasons, Autumn, Casey at the Bat, The Nutcracker, Manny's Mission, Starry Night,* and others. Lisa danced the Sugar Plum Fairy in CPYB's *Nutcracker* in 1975. Lisa continues to teach at New York City Ballet Company and at the CPYB Summer Program. Her father, Andre, is "The Founding Father of CPYB."

Gadzinski, Jessica

Jessica danced Flower, Hot Chocolate, and Coffee in the Nutcracker. She comes to Carlisle from Riverside, California. She is interested in music. Her parents are Josefina and Paul Gadzinski.

Gildea, Cameron Essis

Cameron has studied at CPYB for 6 years. Cameron has had performance roles in: *Peter Pan, June Series, Coppelia, The Nutcracker, Legend of Sleepy Hollow, Madeline, Pandora's Box,* and *Show White.* Her parents are Joni Essis and Cornelius Gildea.

Gildea, Justine Essis

Justine has studied at CPYB for many years. She performed in *Nutcracker, Sleeping Beauty, Pandora's Box, Cinderella's Ball,* and *June Show.* At the Shaull Elementary School she was an Honor Student. Her parents are Joni Essis and Cornelius Gildea.

Gill, Mitch

Mitch is a member of the 'Ballet Family' — father Thomas Gill, mother Theresa Crawford, and Aunt Marcia Dale Weary. Mitch attended Carlisle High School. In the *Nutcracker,* he danced Cavalier, lead Spanish Hot Chocolate. He enjoys playing guitar.

Greene, Abigail

Abigail, 11 year old granddaughter of Haydee Greene, began dance instruction at CPYB at age 3. She has danced in the *Nutcracker, Pandora's Box,* and the *June Show.* Abigail also plays the flute and piano. Grandmother transports her to the "Barn" every day. She attends school in the Big Spring School District - an A student.

Greene, Connor

Connor, 10 year old grandson of Haydee Greene, began dance instruction at CPYB age 3. He has danced in the *Nutcracker, Pandora's Box,* and the *June Show.* Connor also plays trumpet and piano. Grandmother transports him to the "Barn" every day. He attends school in the Big Spring School District - an A student.

Greene, Kate

Kate, 9 year old granddaughter of Haydee Greene, began dance instruction at CPYB at age 3. She has danced in the *Nutcracker, Pandora's Box,* and the *June Show.* Kate also plays the clarinet and piano. Grandmother transports her to the "Barn" every day. She attends school in the Big Spring School District - an A student.

Hirsch, Leah

Leah began to study ballet at CPYB at age 10. She attended the Harrisburg Academy where she was a Scroll Scholar. Leah has performed in CPYB productions of *Nutcracker, Raymonda Variations, Faust, Pas de Quatre,* and *Stars and Stripes.* She is daughter of Donna and Rich Hirsch.

Hoke, Simon

Simon began to study at CPYB at age 7 while a student at Crestview Elementary School. He is involved with Academically Challenging Topics (ACT), and enjoys playing piano, French horn, and singing, as well as computer games and drawing. He has performed in the *Nutcracker, Cinderella, June Show, Peter Pan,* and *Snow White.* He is the son of Christina and Andy Hoke.

Hsieh, Allisyn

Allisyn has been a student at CPYB for four years. At age 18 she danced Sugar Plum Fairy Flower, and Snowflake in *Nutcracker*. She graduated from Carlisle High School, where she was an honor student. She is a member of Amnesty International. She also danced in *Cinderella, Consolation, June Show,* and *Balanchine's Serenade*. She is the daughter of Clare and Lisa Hsich.

Jirard, Jackson

Jackson has studied and danced at CPYB for more than six years. He danced in the *Nutcracker* as Big Mouse, Peter Pan, Toy Soldier, Hot Chocolate, Principal Tea, and Candy Cane. He has also studied and mastered other dance forms including jazz, tap, and contemporary Jackson has competed in a number of state wide competitions. He studied at the Pacific Northwest Ballet summer program in 2009. He danced the lead role in Laszlo Berdo's *Peter Pan* in 2009.

Jurgensen, Susan

Susan joined CPYB at age six with her sister, Heather. Susan progressed in the *Nutcracker* roles from Angel, Clown, Toy Soldier, Candy Cane, Flower, to Snowflake. She performed in Richard Cook's ballets and in all the *June Shows* through her High School Years. She continued to study ballet as an elective course at Rutgers University. Susan is the daughter of Joan and Craig Jurgensen.

Jurgensen, Heather

See below under "Spotlights"

Kubanda, Anastasia

Anastasia has danced with CPYB since age 9. She danced in the *Nutcracker* as Maric, Soldier, Polchinelle, and Columbine. She also plays piano. She also performed in CPYB productions *Cinderella, June Show,* and *Snow White*. Her parents are Stephen and Sharon Kubanda.

LeBlanc, Laurie

Laurie is a native of Rochester, New York. She began her dance training at age 3 in Erie, PA. She studied in Dover, Delaware, with the Regional Ballet. She and the family moved to Dillsburg, Pennsylvania. She then started ballet lessons at CPYB. At age 15, Laurie attended summer SAB in New York City. She then accepted an apprenticeship with The Pennsylvania Ballet, and became a member of the Company the next year.

LeBlanc, Sherri

Sherri trained at CPYB for 12 years. Her professional career started at NYBC, where she danced for 6 years. She then danced for San Francisco Ballet as soloist for 9 years. She performed principal roles in ballets by Robbins, Balanchine, Tharp, Lubovich, Morris, Welch, and Kudelka. She has returned to CPYB to teach in Summer Program and has taught at Orlando Ballet School. She has worked towards a Bachelor of Performing Arts. She and her husband have two sons.

LeBlanc, Tina

See "Spotlights"

Loughran, Kelly

Kelly has studied at CPYB for 3 years. Kelly has had performance roles in: *Peter Pan, The Nutcracker, Coppelia, Snow White,* and *June Series.* Her parents are Thomas and Kenna Loughran.

McAvoy, Caitlin

Caitlin has been studying at CPYB for 3 years. In addition to dance, Caitlin enjoys all music. She began dancing at age 3 in her hometown of Overland Park, Kansas, where she studied tap, jazz, and voice. CPYB performances include: *The Nutcracker, Peter Pan, Snow White, Coppelia,* and *June Series.* Caitlin is the daughter of Matt and Sheryl.

McGowan, Alexander

Alexander has been studying at CPYB a short time. In the Nutcracker he performed the Nutcracker Prince. He is home schooled. He enjoys reading and board games. His parents are Jeanne and Joseph McGowan.

Miller, Ashley

Ashley began to study ballet at CPYB at age 4. She has performed in the *Nutcracker, Legend of Sleepy Hollow, Snow White, Sleeping Beauty,* and *June Show.* She is the daughter of Sandy Kinley and Warren Miller.

Moll, Karl

Karl danced at CPYB for eleven years. He danced in *Nutcracker* as Principal Candy Cane, Tea, Hot Chocolate, Toy Soldier, and Big Mouse. Other roles included: *Russian Character Dance, Dance Macabre, Sleeping Beauty, Cinderella, Snow White,* and *June Shows*. In Carlisle High School, he was involved in Knowledge Masters, German National Honor Society, National Honor Society. He was a Britton Scholar at Dickinson College. He joined the Rochester Ballet professionally in 2009.

Reeder, Brian

Brian was born in Sunbury, Pennsylvania. He began his dance training at CPYB in 1974. He then studied at the American School of Ballet. Brian then danced professionally with New York City Ballet, American Ballet Theater, Ballet Frankfurt (Germany), and Belle Epoque — off Broadway. He has taught Artist in Residence at Brown University, Emory University, St. Paul's School, Alvin Ailey School, and Icelandic National Ballet School. Choreographic works include: *Lady's Choice* (ABT), *Gotcha* (Guggenheim Works), *Loss of Lady C* (PNB), *Peter and the Wolf* (Washington Ballet Studio Company), *The Nutcracker* (Ballet Pacifica), *Vivaldi Variations* (Ballet Academy East), *Waiting Just Waiting* (Emory Univ), and a new work for the Colorado Ballet in 2010. Brian was named by *Time Out New York* as "one of its ten best" for the year 2002 and was selected as "one to watch" by *Dance Magazine* in 2005.

Romeo, Marcus

Marcus has been a student at CPYB for 10 years. In the *Nutcracker*, he danced Cavalier, Candy Cane, Toy Soldier, Big Mouse, and Hot Chocolate. In the Carlisle High School, he was a distinguished honor student. He has danced in major CPYB roles in *Stars and Stripes, Tivinkliana, La Ventrana,* and *de l'innocense*. Marcus performed the role of Nutcracker Prince in 2003, 2004, and 2005. He is the son of John and Beverly Romeo. Marcus was accepted to the School of American Ballet in NYC in 2009.

Romeo, Simone

Simone danced in the *Nutcracker* roles Principal Hot Chocolate, Demi Flower, and Snowflake. She also performed in CPYB productions *Raymonda Variations, Stars and Stripes,*

Walspurgisnacht, La Bayadere, Sleeping Beauty, and *Legend of Sleepy Hollow.* She is daughter of John and Beverly Romeo.

Rowe, Julia

Julia has danced at CPYB for ten years. In *Nutcracker,* she danced Sugar Plum Fairy, Dew Drop. She also performed in *Who Cares?, Legend of Sleepy Hollow, Sleeping Beauty,* and *Divertimento No. 15.* She was an honor student at Cumberland Valley High School. Her parents are Thomas and Susan Rowe.

Smith, Julia

Julia is a freshman at Shippensburg University where she majors in mathematics. CPYB performances include: *The Nutcracker, Serenade, Raynonda, La Source, Faust, Stars and Stripes, Coppelia, Cinderella, Rococo, Counter Poses, Paquita,* and *La Bayadere.* Julia's parents are Brent and Sharon Smith. She dedicates her dance to Mema and Nana.

Snyder, Grace

Grace has studied at CPYB since age 4. In the *Nutcracker,* she has danced Sugarplum Fairy, Principal Shepherdess, Snowflake, Tea, Columbine, and Demi Flower. She has also performed principal roles in *Snow White, Madeline, Cinderella, Raymonda Variations, Pas de Quatre, Sleeping Beauty, Stars and Stripes, Walspurgisnacht, Tivinkliana, Pandora's Box,* and *Legend of Sleepy Hollow.* She is the daughter of Cynthia and Garry Snyder.

Sweigart, Matthew

Matthew began to study at CPYB in 2008 in the summer program. Age 21, Matthew is a graduate of American Musical and Dramatic Academy. In addition to ballet, he enjoys tap, jazz, singing, and acting. Past performances at CPYB include *Peter Pan.* He hopes for a career in dancing.

Villella, Michael

Michael danced at CPYB for three years. In the *Nutcracker,* he danced Cavalier, Principal Tea, Principal Hot Chocolate, Father, and Big Mouse. He also performed in CPYB productions *Sleeping Beauty, Cinderella, Stars and Stripes, Vienna Life,* and *June Shows.* He is the son of Robert and Linda Villella.

Walborn, Sarah

Sarah danced in the CPYB *Nutcracker* as Sugar Plum Fairy, Dewdrop, Coffee, and Snowflake. She studied at CPYB for ten years. Sarah joined San Francisco Ballet in 2007 where she performed in *Symphony in C, Don Quixote, Firebird, Wheeldon's Carousel, Robbins' West Side Story Suite,* and Balanchine's *Serenade*, and others.

Whitesel, Donna Gregor

Donna was a student at the Marcia Dale School of Dance in the 1960s. During her initial ballet training, she danced with some of the first graduates who would become professional dancers: Lisa de Ribere, Michael Owen, Sean Lavery, and Marcia Darhower. She also attended Saturday training sessions at the Pennsylvania Ballet where she studied under Barbara Weisberger. At age 14, and standing 5'10", close to her tall father, (see "A Tall Story") she decided not to become a ballet dancer. Her dance career instead branched out to encompass choreography and ultimately teaching. Her excellent training under Marcia Dale Weary provided a basis on which to teach tap, theater dance, modern dance, as well as ballet. Along the way she obtained a BS degree in Early Childhood Education, which was a strong foundation for teaching young students. Her ultimate dream of starting a Marcia-style school was realized when she founded DanceWorks, LLC in the small prairie town of Nebraska City, Nebraska in 2001. A small mid western school, Donna regularly attracted 110 dance students each year. In 2003, she founded the Arbor Dance Company, a non-profit performing company, dedicated to quality ballet performance and collaboration with other artists. Donna eventually became certified in the Cecchetti Ballet method, a widely recognized system of teaching classical ballet. More than one hundred of her student graduates have passed certifying exams with high honors, typically traveling long distances by corn fields and through mid western blizzards to demonstrate their dedication and commitment. The year 2010 marks the 10th anniversary of Dance Works, a school where every plie, pirouette, and actual performance represents the founding methods and spirit of Marcia Dale Weary. That Donna generates and administers a successful school of classical ballet in a small mid western community is a tribute to Donna herself.

Wilmarth, Emma

Emma has been studying at CPYB for 6 years. Emma's interests include art, sewing, scrapbooking. Her past performances include: *The Nutcracker, June Series, Coppelia, Snow White, Madeline,* and *Pandora's Box.* Emma's parents are John and Fiona Wilmarth.

Zahorian, Vanessa

Interview in the CPYB June Series booklet of June 2010: Question: What advice do you have for students hoping to become dancers? Vanessa: "Be patient. Kismet, as my father tells me. No matter what obstacles and challenges come your way, life is a learning experience. As principal dancer with the San Francisco Ballet (2010), I'm still learning. I enjoy every moment."

STAFF, FACULTY, ADMINISTRATION

Allwein, Katrina
Katrina has a Bachelor of Fine Arts degree from Point Park University. She studied at CPYB and has been teaching for 20 plus years.

Alsedek, Anne
(Drama for Dancers) Anne has been teaching Drama for Dancers at CPYB since 1994. She is Education Director at Open Stage of Harrisburg (PA), and is the Program Director of the Capital Area School for the Arts. Anne is also a professional actress and director, and has appeared in numerous plays and musicals, including the role of the Stepmother in CPYB *Cinderella*. Her brother is Sean Lavery, Assistant to New York City Ballet's Master-in-Chief, Peter Martins.

Baker, Beth
Beth has been dancing for over 30 years. She has a Bachelor's degree in Exercise Science with a concentration in Dance. She has danced professionally with Orchesis. Ms. Baker's style of modern dance and jazz is based on core strengthening, body awareness, and fun.

Berdo, Laszlo
Laszlo was born in Grand Rapids, Michigan, where he began dancing at age 5. Mr. Berdo later intensified his studies at the National Academy of Arts in Champaign, Illinois. Upon graduation he joined Ballet Austin and then Louisville Ballet under Alun Jones and Helen Starr. He was then hired by Ivan Nagy as soloist with the Cincinnati Ballet. Mr. Berdo then joined the Boston Ballet in 1990. He became principal in 1995. Laszlo was the first to perform the lead role in Cranko's *Eugene Onegin* in the US. He began to choreograph in 1993, and created *Eternal Being* for the Boston Ballet. In 1997, he was commissioned to create a new work - *Four Hands* - for Boston Ballet. In 1999, Berdo created *Below Down Under* which premiered at the Schubert Theater. In 2001, he created *Sanctuary* for the Norwegian National Ballet in Oslo. Berdo choreographed *Bass Elements* for the Boston Ballet and participated in Choreoplan 2001 in which he

created *Concertante* for CPYB. Berdo's pas de deux's have been performed in galas in Helsinki, St. Petersburg, and Budapest. He also choreographed multiple solos for contestants at the Jackson International Ballet competition as well as the Youth American Grand Prix. He choreographed *Peter Pan* for CPYB - which premiered in October 2009. Laszlo was commissioned to choreograph a ballet to represent the Frederick Hart sculpture *Daughters of Odessa* for the CPYB Gala in October 2009.

Cook, Richard
See "The Cook Book"

Comeau, Maia
Maia is a graduate of Carlisle High School and Penn State University. She studied ballet for ten years at CPYB. Maia was a member of Complexions Dance Company in 2000. She has performed in Balanchine's *Nutcracker* (Frau Stahlbaum), *Valse Francaise, Divertimento No. 15*, and *Walspurgisnacht*. She works for the German Marshall Fund of the United States in Washington, DC. She was elected to the Board of CPYB in 2008.

Crawford, Theresa
Theresa Lee Crawford is a niece of Marcia Dale Weary. As a toddler, she lived in Carlisle, enjoyed the atmosphere of "the Barn" and even performed a street scene role in a performance of the early Marcia Dale School of Dance. Although the Crawford family moved to Michigan when Theresa was two, the family would return regularly to Carlisle for vacations and ballet performances. Theresa began her travels from Michigan to Carlisle to study with her Aunt Marcia during the summers. Under the tutelage of her Aunt, Theresa began assisting Marcia in class from a young age. With Marcia's assistance, Theresa actually started a school of her own at age 14 in Travers City, Michigan. Marcia of course, has been instrumental in Theresa's development as a teacher. Marcia served occasionally as a teacher in Theresa's school and even produced choreographic works as a gift. Theresa founded a non-profit children's ballet company – The Michigan Youth Ballet - in 1981, She herself has served as guest instructor in Michigan, Missouri, Virginia, and Pennsylvania. She became a member of CPYB faculty in 1995, where she has choreographed original pieces. Ms. Crawford is also a faculty member of the Hershey School of Dance. She is currently Artistic

Advisor of the South School of the Orlando Ballet, Florida. Theresa first met Thomas Gill at CPYB during the Summer Program in 1971. The two met again at a CPYB Stars performance in July 2005- and MARRIED.

Eppley, Sara

Originally from Buffalo, New York, Sara is an alum of CPYB. She first studied Cecchetti Method of ballet and is I.S.T.D. certified for levels 1 thru 4. She has performed with the Buffalo Ballet Theater, Thousand Islands Festival Ballet Company, and the Lake Erie Ballet. She has also participated in the Carlisle Project Workshop. She is certified by New York City Ballet to teach the New York City Ballet Workout. In addition to teaching, Ms. Eppley was previously on the faculty of the Cincinnati Ballet and Tanze Performing Arts Center in Ohio.

Fields, Ann

Ann has a Bachelor of Fine Arts degree in ballet from the University of Utah. She has danced with Lake Erie Ballet in conjunction with Mercyhurst College and with the Utah Ballet. She has completed teaching apprenticeships with Sharon Filone at the School of the Lake Erie Ballet and with University of Utah. Ms. Fields is an alum of CPYB. She is also certified by New York City Ballet to teach the New York City Ballet Workout.

Good, Alecia

Alecia Good, former principal dancer with the Kansas City Ballet, began her dancing career with Marcia at the Central Pennsylvania Youth Ballet in 1969 at the age of five primarily as an outlet for her over abundance of energy, according to her parents. At the age of nine, Alecia received her first pair of pointe shoes and her love affair with ballet was born. From 1976-1978 she attended the School of American Ballet's summer program followed by three summers at the Joffrey Ballet on full scholarship. While studying with Marcia, Alecia danced the lead in Balanchine's *Tchaikovsky Pas de Deux, Con Amore*, the Snow Queen in *The Nutcracker* and more. In 1981, she left Carlisle to further her training at the Pennsylvania Ballet on full scholarship where she remained until 1983 when she accepted her first professional job with the Kansas City Ballet. As a principal dancer with the Kansas City Ballet, Alecia had the privilege to perform many lead roles such as Swanilda in *Coppelia*, Aurora in the *Sleeping Beauty*, Snow Queen and Sugar Plum in the *Nutcracker*, George Balanchine's *Firebird, The Four Temperaments, Concerto Barrocco, Apollo* and *Western Symphony*. Alecia is currently on staff at the Kansas City Ballet School and is the Director of the Kansas City Youth Ballet, a student company to the Kansas City Ballet. She has been featured in several Hallmark "Ballerina" calendars and has been listed in the book of "Who's who in America's Teachers." Alecia has guest taught throughout the midwest and has been returning to CPYB to teach in the Summer Session for the past 20 years.

Grigorian, Rafael

Rafael was trained at the Baku Choreographic Institute and at the Kirov Ballet School in Leningrad/St. Petersburg, Russia under the instruction of A. I. Pushkin. For twenty years he was a principal dancer with the Baku Theater of Opera and Ballet. In 1980, Mr. Grigorian was awarded Laureate of the State of the USSR, and received the very prestigious title of the People's Artist of Azerbaijan. He toured extensively in Europe and Asia with stars of the Kirov and Bolshoi Ballet Theaters. He served as instructor of the Moscow Ballet Festival under the leadership of soloist S. Radchenko. From 1986 until 1991, he held the title of Choreographer for the Moscow School of Ice Dancing. He immigrated to the United States in 1991. He then opened a School of Classical Ballet in Corning, New York. In 1993, Rafael was asked by Marcia Dale Weary of the CPYB to teach in the Summer School Program. Mr. Grigorian then founded the Rafael Grigorian Ballet Theater. In 1996, he received the prestigious Arts Partnership Award of the Southern Finger Lakes for his outstanding contribution to the arts of the Southern Tier Communities.

Hench, Leslie

Leslie was Marcia's first student in 1956 when classes were held in the Carlisle Town Band building on South Street. Leslie advanced, and later studied at The School of American Ballet in NYC. She then danced with the Harlequin Ballet in London. She began teaching at CPYB in 1965. She assisted Marcia in the establishment of a Harrisburg Ballet studio – where Sean Lavery was a student. Her daughter, Tara Hench, and son, Zachary Hench, both studied at CPYB and went on to professional careers with Boston Ballet and Pennsylvania Ballet. Tara is married to Laszlo Berdo, CPYB faculty. Leslie continued to teach and coach at CPYB until 2009.

Hench, Tara

Tara originates from Loysville, PA. She received ballet training at Central Pennsylvania Youth Ballet, School of American Ballet, and Kirov Academy. Ms. Hench danced with the Boston Ballet for 11 years. She is also Pilates certified. She and her husband, Laszlo, have a son - Noah.

Hench, Zachary

Zachary began his training at 7 at CPYB. After studying for eight years, he trained further at the Kirov Academy in Washington D.C. He became a member of Boston Ballet in 1993. While there he danced principal roles in *Swan Lake, Firebird*, and others. In 2000 he joined San Francisco Ballet and became principal in 2003. He joined Pennsylvania Ballet in 2004 where he has dance lead roles in ballets of Wheeldon, Cranko, Ashton, Tharp, Robbins, and Balanchine.

Hineline, Alan

Alan Hineline was born in Franklin, Ohio. He trained in dance with Dance Theater Dayton, Milton Myers, and David Howard. Company affiliations include Eglevsky, Nashville Ballet, Joyce Trisler Company, and Laura Dean Dancers. He came to CPYB initially in 1995 for a dance assignment. In 1997, at the invitation of Marcia Dale Weary, Alan was named Resident Choreographer of Central Pennsylvania Youth Ballet. The numerous ballets which Alan has created include: *Sans Souci, Chopin Departures, Take Me Out to the Ballet, Legend of Sleepy Hollow, The Many Tales of Madeline, Cinderella's Ball, Cinderella, The Sleeping Beauty, Rococo Variations, Adieu Waltzes, de l'innocense, Madeline and the Gypsies,* and others. His body of work can be seen in the repertoires of American Ballet Theater Studio Company, Pennsylvania Ballet, Atlanta Ballet, Dayton Ballet, Kansas City Ballet, Julliard Dance Ensemble, Sacramento Ballet, Alabama Ballet, Ballet Concierto de Cuba, Utah Regional Ballet, and others. As teacher, Mr. Hineline has instructed every level of dancer. He has been guest faculty for Richmond Ballet, Atlanta Ballet, Julliard School, and others. He has taught at the Aoyama Festival, and numerous colleges across the US. Mr. Hineline sits on the national advisory Board of Regional Dance America. He is the founder of CPYB's Choreoplan. Among his many awards are the Choo-San Goh Award for Choreography and multiple awards from Regional Dance America. Mr. Hineline was Artistic

Director of Ballet Philippines for the year 2007-2008. He was selected Chief Executive Officer of the Central Pennsylvania Youth Ballet in July 2009.

Hoover, Darla

See "Darla-ing of CPYB"

Howe, Melinda

Melinda has served on the CPYB faculty for over twenty years. She began her studies in ballet with Marcia in 1975. She received a Bachelor of Fine Arts from the North Carolina School of the Arts, and then returned to CPYB. Her growth as a teacher has led her to teach and choreograph with other companies - Cumberland Dance, Allegheny Ballet. Ms. Howe received the Northeast Regional Dance America and Monticello Awards for choreography in *Andante*. Her ballet, *Vivaldi*, was performed at the RDA Festival in 1999. Another work, *Esprit*, was done at the RDA Gala performance in 2005.

Intrieri, Anita

Anita began her dance training at CPYB in 1975. She is a graduate of the North Carolina School of the Arts. She has danced in various companies such as North Carolina Dance Theater, Ballet Hispancio of New York, and Lar Lubovitch Dance Company. She has also danced on Broadway with "Phantom of the Opera, Red Shoes, and Cabaret." Currently, Anita is on faculty at the Logrea Dance Academy in Ossining, New York. She teaches in CPYB Summer Program.

Lawyer, Shellie

Shellie began her dance career at an early age, and studied ballet, jazz, tap, and hip hop. Following high school, Ms. Lawyer became a professional cheerleader. She was later contracted by Arthur Murray as a ballroom and Latin dance instructor. She continues to teach dance independently as well as at CPYB.

LeBlanc, Shirley

Shirley is the proud mother of Laurie, Russell, Tina, and Sherri LeBlanc - all of whom attended CPYB. Shirley had a career as nurse anesthetist while she transported and nurtured all her children to Carlisle six days per week for ballet classes. She in addition volunteered at CPYB for committee work, dressing during performances, and fund raising. Shirley taught Marcia how to drive an automobile! She currently lives in Nevada with husband Russell. Shirley has been a pillar of strength and support to her family.

Monroe, Josh

Lighting Designer: Josh's credits include *Thwak* at the Peacock Theater; *Sensuous Woman* at the Zipper Theater; *Monster* at the New Village Gate Theater; *Winter Explosion* for Alvin Ailey School; *Cinderella* for Point Park University; *Legend of Sleepy Hollow* for Alabama Ballet; *Nutcracker* for CPYB; and many others.

Nash, David

Production Staff: As a dancer, David toured extensively with the Milwaukee Ballet, Ballet Met, Dance Kaleidoscope, Pittsburgh Ballet, and Limon Dance Company. As principal stage manager for the Joffrey Ballet, David toured more that 100 ballets throughout the United States. He and his wife, Susan, established Stow/Nash Associates a theater consulting firm based in Pittsburgh. David has provided arts planning and design consultation to numerous performing institutions, including Broadway. He designed the digital/HDTV-ready television studio at Point Park University. David serves on the Disability Agenda 2000 Task Force for Inclusion. He is also adjunct instructor in dance and theater at Point Park University.

Ninos, Karen Bohner

Karen studied ballet during the 1960s at the Marcia Dale School of Dance in Harrisburg. With that foundation, Karen founded the Campbelltown School of Ballet in 1979. Later she founded and directed the Alfred Ballet Academy in 1988. She choreographed over 22 original ballets for students in her ballet schools. She was formerly dance faculty at Alfred University in Alfred, NY. She was also personal assistant to Robert Joffrey of the Joffrey Ballet (NYC). She won the Monticello Choreographers Award. For 30 years she has been on the faculty of the CPYB Summer Program.

Rabassi-Davis, AnnaMarie "Re"

"Re" holds a Bachelor of Arts degree in Ballet Education, and trained as an apprentice teacher with the Royal Winnipeg Ballet. She completed the teacher training course with Jacque D'Amboise National Dance Institute. Formerly the founder and Director of the Gettysburg School of Ballet, she also served on the faculty of Mt. St. Mary's College as Choreographer and the Harrisburg Arts Magnet

School. During this time she created and implemented the Creative Movement and Pre-Ballet curriculum that been used at CPYB. Ms. Rabassi-Davis developed the Foundation for the Arts in Education program and created the dance curriculum for the Capital Area School of the Arts. She also holds a M.Ed. degree from Shippensburg University in Counseling and an M.S. in Business Ethics and Leadership from Duquesne University. She currently teaches Drama and Dance at Milton Hershey School while serving as permanent faculty for the academic and Summer Programs at CPYB since 1984. She is artistic coordinator for the CPYB Discover Dance program. She served as Guidance Counselor at William Penn Middle School from '96-'99. "Re" is preparing a Teaching Manual for Pre-Ballet which was piloted at Spartanburg Ballet. To be published in 2010.

Reed, Jason

Jason began taking ballet lessons at CPYB at age 18. Following High School graduation, he entered the Julliard School in New York City. He obtained a BFA degree in Dance in 2000. He founded the outreach program REACH which offers academic, recreational and inspirational dance to children with social and academic needs. Jason has also worked in dance programs with Rebecca Wright and at the Ballet Tech with Eliot Feld. He has also provided outreach programs with the New York City Department of Education. Jason was appointed Director of CPYB Outreach Program in September 2009.

Riseling, Jonathan

Jonathan graduated from the High School for the Performing Arts in New York City and received the celebrated Helen Tamiris Award. He was invited to join the Alvin Ailey Repertory Ensemble and was later accepted into the Alvin Ailey Dance Theater. He then danced with a number of other companies. He also worked with Judith Jamison and assisted her with choreography and staging in the Jamison Project in 1998. In 1990 he was awarded a "Bessie Award." He has also taught at the Alvin Ailey Dance Center, STEPS ON Broadway, Danspace, Peridance, Ballet Hispanico, and Ballet Academy East in New York City, and Central Pennsylvania Youth Ballet.

Smith, Betty

Betty came to CPYB in 2006. She brings more than 25 years of experience - many of these with Alabama Ballet Company. Her creations have been used around the world by many dance companies and at international competitions. She has worked with numerous dance companies - including Ballet West, Miami City Ballet, Colorado Ballet, Ballet Dallas, San Antonio Ballet, American Ballet Theater II. Betty has worked with Mikhail Baryshnikov on his One Man Show. She has served on the staff of the Alabama School of Fine Arts, the Jillana School, and others. She has taught costuming at the United States Institute for Theatre Technology, Inc. Ms. Smith is listed in the Metropolitan Who's Who and is a member of the Costume Society of America.

Sorrell, Patricia

Pat began her dancing training in California with Theodore Kosloff and Alexandra Baldina. As a young dancer, she performed with the California Opera Company and the Gollner-Petroff Company. She did commercial work in movies and television and spent a season doing aerial work in the Terrell Jacobs Circus. After moving to the East coast, Pat danced with the Washington Ballet and the National Ballet under Frederic Franklin. This was followed by tours as a stage manager and stagehand to "learn how things go backstage." Ms. Sorrell is currently based in Norfolk, Virginia where she is Artistic Advisor and faculty member with Ballet Virginia International. She also directs the children's performing company "First Pointe Players." In 1970, Pat came to see Edward Myers perform at Central Pennsylvania Youth Ballet. She spent an inspirational evening decorating Coppelia dolls with Marcia Dale Weary. That began a long association with Marcia and the CPYB. She has done original choreography and staging for *Giselle, Coppelia, Cinderella, Paquita,* and *Nutcracker.* Pat has returned to Carlisle regularly for many years to teach, support, and advise in the Summer Program.

Stafford, Abi

Abi began studying ballet at Central Pennsylvania Youth Ballet at age six under Marcia Dale Weary in 1988. During her ten year course, she performed in many of the choreographic works of Marcia Dale Weary, George Balanchine, Alan Hineline, Gennadi Vostrikov, and Richard Cook. She did lead roles as Sugar Plum Fairy and Dewdrop in the *Nutcracker* and also Liberty Bell in Balanchine's *Stars and Stripes*. Abi performed during tours of CPYB to Tokyo (Japan), Houston (Texas), Jackson (Mississippi), as well as to many theater venues across the state of Pennsylvania. In 1998, Abi entered the School of American Ballet in New York City. She joined the New York City Ballet Company in 1999, and was promoted to principal dancer in 2007.

Stafford, Jonathan

Born in Carlisle, PA, Jonathan began his dance training at age 8 with CPYB. He entered the School of American Ballet in 1997. Mr. Stafford joined the New York City Ballet Company in 1998. He was promoted to principal dancer in 2006. He has danced featured roles in *Firebird, Nutcracker, Midsummer Night's Dream,* Martins' *Octet,* Robbins' *Fancy Free, Fanfare,* and Wheeldon's *Polyphonia,* Mr. Stafford received the Martin Segal Award from SAB in 1999. He has also danced in films, Center Stage. His sister is Abi Stafford, NYCB Soloist. Jonathan became the Artistic Director of the New York City Ballet in 2019.

Summers, Scott

Technical Director: Scott obtained a BS degree in Quantitative Business Analysis in 1987. He volunteered as a stage hand at the Whitaker Center in Harrisburg- and discovered the art of stage and lighting design. He became a professional technical director - and subsequently designed stages for Neville Brothers, Wynton Marsalis, and then big productions of *Cat on A Hot Tin Roof, Candide, Chicago, Barber of Seville*. He also designs sets for Premier Production Services, which produces conventions and other large business meetings.

Thornton, Bruce

Bruce received his dance training in his native Seattle at the Cornish Institute. He later trained at the Central Pennsylvania Youth Ballet from 1988-1991. He danced with the Miami City Ballet where he was soloist - from 1991 until 2006. He danced a range of roles, including the "*Blue Gentleman*" from *Robbins' Dances at a Gathering,* the "walking" pas de deux from *Emeralds,* the *Elegie* principal from *Serenade*, the principal male in *Concerto Barrocco*, the role of Death in *La Valse,* the Baron in *La Sonnambula,* first and third themes from *The Four Temperaments* (all Balanchine). He has a wide experience with Paul Taylor, Richard Tanner, Margo Sappington, Sir Frederick Ashton, August Bournonville, and Edward Villella. He has performed as guest artist for Carolina Ballet in TV performances of *Romeo and Juliet* and *Cabaret* at Café Marcovici. He performed for President Bill Clinton in a televised performance at the Kennedy Center. Mr. Thornton brought his expertise in the Balanchine repertoire and his years of experience with the great Edward Villella to the CPYB faculty in January 2007.

Vostrikov, Gennadi

Gennadi was born in Siberia, Russia. He received his early training in Perm. He studied ballet with the renowned teachers Plaht and Asaular. Gennadi was awarded the first degree diploma in the Leningrad Ballet Competition. Upon graduation, he joined the Moiseyev Classical Ballet Company. He was coached by the legendary masters Igor Moiseyev, Asaff Messerer, and Sulamif Messerer. The Moiseyev Ballet Theater traveled worldwide. While on tour, he defected to Mexico. While dancing with the Mexico Ballet Company he was asked by Nicholas Petrov to join the Pittsburgh Ballet Company. He stared as soloist in *Nutcracker, Prince Igor, Rite of Spring, Coppelia, Cinderella, Swan Lake, Don Quixote,* and many others. Mr. Vostrikov was also principal dancer with Chicago Ballet. He was asked by Marcía Dale Weary to join CPYB as guest teacher in the Summer Program in 1971. In 1982 he founded the Virginia Academy of Ballet. He then formed the Virginia Youth Ballet Company in 1989. He continues to teach dance and choreography at Shenandoah University. He has done guest teaching at Pittsburgh Ballet School, Williamsburg Chamber Ballet, New Castle Ballet, and at the National Regional Ballet Festivals.

Vostrikov, Susan

Susan is the co-director of Vostrikov's Academy of Ballet in Winchester, Virginia, and the Virginia Youth Ballet. She is also ballet mistress of the Maracaibo Ballet in Venezuela. She is a former principal dancer with the Milwaukee Ballet, Chicago Ballet, Pittsburgh Ballet, and Ballet UAB.

Weary, Marcia Dale

Marcia began her teaching career in Carlisle in 1955 after her studies with Thalia Mara and Arthur Mahoney at the School of Ballet

Repertory in New York City. Her unequaled dedication to her school and students have brought CPYB to the top of the dance field. The New York Times stated in 1989 that Weary is "considered one of the country's foremost ballet teachers." Ms. Weary is the 1992 recipient of the Distinguished Service to the Arts Award for Central Pennsylvania. She and the CPYB have been featured in leading newspapers, magazines, and television features, and in the award-wining documentary film presented on National Public Television - Children with a Dream. In May 2009, she received the Distinguished Citizen Award from the Pennsylvania Society - presented by Leroy Zimmerman. Marcia died on March 4, 2019.

Whitaker, Kelly

Kelly is a native of Cincinnati, Ohio. She currently dances professionally and teaches ballet in Columbia, South Carolina. She studied in Cincinnati with Daniel Simmons and Nancy Fountain. She has danced soloist roles for Columbia City Ballet and Contemporary Ballet Theater. She has taught yoga at CPYB since 2003. She has also studied Ashtanga and Sport Yoga and its benefits to dance.

Wolfe, Amanda

Amanda is certified as a Pilates Mat Teacher through Fitour Fitness Instruction Training. For more than 15 years Ms. Wolfe studied ballet in Pennsylvania schools - including Rock School of the Pennsylvania Ballet, Pennsylvania Academy of Ballet, and CPYB. During a European tour, she trained with the Viennese dance School Tanz Forum. Amanda graduated from York College of Pennsylvania in 2002, with a Bachelor degree in History. She currently works in the office of Human Resources for Harisburg School District.

SPOTLIGHTS
Master stories in:

ADMINISTRATION

Wingard, Maurinda
Obituary:

On March 29, 2009, CPYB lost its Executive Director – Maurinda C. Wingard, after a long and courageous battle with cancer. Maurinda leaves behind an unparalleled legacy that will benefit CPYB for years to come. Maurinda found her passion for the arts at the young age of six, when she began her dance training with Marcia Dale Weary at Central Pennsylvania Youth Ballet. Upon graduation from CPYB, she attended Skidmore College, where she continued her dance training with several former ballerinas. She later moved to the West coast to work in San Francisco's financial district. Six years later, the East coast drew her back into the dance world. She became administrator for the Carlisle Project, a national choreographic project funded by the Ford Foundation. After nine successful years with this prestigious arts organization, Maurinda accepted a position as Project Manager for the Physics Workshop Project at Dikinson College. She concurrently studied and obtained a Bachelor's Degree from Dickinson, summa cum laude. With her strong background as a dancer, administrator, and arts professional, she was selected to become the Executive Director of CPYB in 1997. During her tenure, both CPYB's annual operating budget and physical plant tripled in size - with the addition of new rehearsal studios in a renovated warehouse on the Dickinson campus. In addition, CPYB was appointed Resident Ballet Company at the Whitaker Center for Science and the Arts in Harrisburg, Pennsylvania. Maurinda expressed her love of dance and her dedication to CPYB in many ways. The Maurinda Wingard New Hope Scholarship Fund was established to honor the life of Maurinda and to keep her vision of CPYB moving forward.

ARTISTIC DIRECTOR

Lavery, Sean

Sean Lavery was born in Harrisburg, Pennsylvania, and began his ballet training at the age of ten at the Marcia Dale School of Dance. Later he studied at the Pennsylvania Ballet School, and in 1968 he appeared as the *Nutcracker* Prince in the premier of that company's production of the *Nutcracker*. Soon after, Mr. Lavery moved to New York to continue his studies with Richard Thomas and Barbara Fallis at the New York School of Ballet, while completing his academic education at the Professional Children's School. Mr. Lavery first danced in George Balanchine's ballets when he joined San Francisco Ballet in 1973. He then danced with the Frankfurt Opera Ballet (Germany) in 1975. In 1976, Mr. Lavery returned to New York and began classes at the School of American Ballet, the official school of the New York City Ballet Company. He was invited to join the Company in 1977, and his debut role was as Titania's Cavalier in Balanchine's *A Midsummer Night's Dream*. He was promoted to soloist in early 1976, and then to principal dancer later that year. Mr. Lavery originated roles in Balanchine's *Waltzes Vienna* and *Kammermusik No. 2*; Jerome Robbins' *Concertino* and *I'm Old Fashioned*; Peter Martins' *A Schubertiad*. His large repertoire included *Apollo, Chaconne, Concerto Barocco, Divertimento N.15, Gounod Symphony, Jewels, La Source, Symphony in C, Mozartiana, Who Cares?, Afternoon of a Faun, Dances at a Gathering,* and many others. Mr. Lavery has often appeared on television. He performed in two of the "Dance American/Choreography by Balanchine" programs for PBS, and for several years performed on "Gala of Stars."

After retiring from dancing in 1986, Mr. Lavery hosted the Dancers Emergency Fund Benefit (1988) and directed the Saratoga Springs Choreography Project (1988). In 1989, Mr. Lavery was promoted to the position of Assistant to the Ballet Master-in-Chief of NYCB. His duties include teaching Company class, staging ballets, and assisting Peter Martins in the preparation of programs and season schedules. He teaches and directs at the School of American Ballet.

In 1989, Mr. Lavery taught at Barnard College and choreographed an original piece for Barnard students - *Twinkliana*. In 1991, Sean choreographed the balcony scene from *Romeo and Juliet* for a special performance for the Dancers' Emergency Fund Benefit. Mr. Lavery's other choreographic credits include *Aurora's Wedding* (1998) and *Classical Symphony* (1999) for Ballet Florida. In addition, Sean staged Balanchine ballets for the George Balanchine Trust. Sean Lavery died in 2018.

PERFORMANCE

LeBlanc, Tina

{Dance Magazine, March 2006, by Allan Ulrich}

At best, judging dancers by their national origin is a fool's game. But who can resist playing it when the dancer is Tina LeBlanc? Watch her perform for 20 minutes and you will know why she is the quintessential American ballerina. The purity of her line, the directness of her gesture, the clarity of her articulation, the vulnerability with which she permits the music to engulf her limbs, and the sheer naturalness of her demeanor – all betoken the guilelessness of this country at its finest. LeBlanc's biography offers no contradiction. She was trained entirely on native soil {CPYB}, launched her professional career in association with one major American dance institution, the Joffrey Ballet, and has attained her glorious peak in another the San Francisco Ballet, which LeBlanc does not hesitate to call "the best company in the country." Except for raising a family, there has been nothing else. Her star has risen high in the sky and remains there, radiating a luster that remains undimmed even now in her late 30s. (*Dance Magazine*, Allan Ulrich; 3/06)

Tina trained at CPYB from 1975. She joined the Joffrey Ballet in 1984. She then began her career with the San Francisco Ballet in 1992 Lead roles included: *Giselle, Swan Lake, Sleeping Beauty, Romeo and Juliet Nutcracker, Quartette,* and *Don Quixote*. She created roles in *Bartok, Quartette Criss-Cross, Angelo and Night, The Dance House,* Wheeldon's *Quaternary*. Other principal roles include *Prism, Chaconne for Piano and Two Dancers Landers' Etudes*; Balanchine's *Theme and Variations, Symphony in C, Apollo and Rubies*; Robbins' *Dances at a Gathering*; Flindt's *The Lesson*. Her honors include two Isadora Duncan Dance Awards and Princess Grace Statuette Award (1995). Tina retired from San Francisco Ballet in June 2009 – with Marcia Dale Weary proudly seated in the audience.

TEACHER

Weary, Marcia Dale

Standing at the podium at Gettysburg's Majestic Theater in 2006 to receive the Governor's Award for the Arts, with Pennsylvania Governor Edward Rendell at her side, and 500 people in the audience, Marcia stretches up to the microphone to speak, and responds in typical modesty "Thank you for the honor. It's my students who are great. I'm just a teacher." And a teacher she's been - personally for 60 of her 75 years and professionally for 55 years as director of the Central Pennsylvania Youth Ballet. More than a teacher though, Marcia has been a mentor, a person builder, a counselor, a matriarch to legions of children and students. Her awards put some of this celebrity into words - Distinguished Service to the Arts Award in 1992, the Carlisle Regional Arts Award in 2000, and the Distinguished Citizen Award of The Pennsylvania Society in May 2009. Marcia recalls sentimentally that "my father wanted me to be an artist. Truly speaking, Marcia Dale, daughter of Dale, is in every sense of the word a true Artist.

WORLD TOUR

Jurgensen, Heather

Heather set out on her World Tour of ballet in "The Barn" in Carlisle, Pennsylvania. She then ventured forth to New York City where she trained at The School of American Ballet. The next trip was across the street to the New York State Theater - where she danced with the New York City Ballet Company (1986). Then on to Europe and a flight across the Atlantic to Hamburg, Germany to start a twenty year career with the Hamburg Ballet Company (1989). An actual ballet performance of The Odyssey by Director Choreographer John Neumeier was to portend travels with the Hamburg Ballet Company around the world. Passport entries from 1989 until 2007 include (alphabetically):

Aix-en-Province	Oberammergau
Athens	Osaka
Baden-Baden	Palermo
Basel (Switz)	Paris
Beijing	Prague
Belfast (Ireland)	Rio de Janeiro
Bern (Switz)	Rome
Brisbane (Australia)	Rostock
Buenos Aires	Salzburg
Copenhagen	Sao Paolo
Donetsk (Ukraine)	Sapporo
Donetsk	Shanghai
Dresden	Singapore
Faro (Portugal)	Stuttgart
Frankfurt	St. Barthelemy
Fukuoka	St. Petersburg, Russia
Hamburg	St. Polton (Austria)
Hiroshima	Stockholm
Hong Kong	Tokyo, Japan
Kiev	Torino
Kobe (Japan)	Toronto (Canada)
Los Angeles	Toulon (France)
Lvov (Ukraine)	Vaison la Romaine
Madrid	Vienna
Moscow	Washington, DC
Munich	Yokohama
Nagoya	York (England)
New York	

Heather became the Co-Director of Ballet Kiel in Germany with her partner, Yaroslav Ivanenko in 2010.

Professional Dancers
CPYB
PROFESSIONAL ALUMNI, 2009

SAN FRANCISCO BALLET
  Tina LeBlanc
  Vanessa Zahorian
  Kristen Long
NEW YORK CITY BALLET
  Ashley Bouder
  Abi Stafford
  Jonathan Stafford
  Allen Peiffer
  Adam Hendrickson
  Tabitha Rinko-Gay
  Stephanie Chrosniak
BOSTON BALLET
  Lia Cirio
  Kathleen Combes
PENNSYLVANIA BALLET
  Zachery Hench
  Tara Hench
  Ian Hussey
  Victoria Gates
  Rachel Maher
CINCINNATI BALLET
  Mishic Corn
ASPEN/SANTA FE
  Luke Willis
PACIFIC NORTHWEST BALLET
  Carrie Imler
  Robbie-Jean Arbott
  Noelani Pantastico
  Kara Zimmerman
LOUISVILLE BALLET
  Lara Bricker
MIAMI CITY BALLET
  Callie Manning
  Bruce Thornton
  Elise McKinley
PAUL TAYLOR
  Jamie Walker
MILWAUKEE BALLET
  Jennifer Miller
BALLET AUSTRALIA
  Jennifer Provins
HAMBURG BALLET
  Heather Jurgensen
AMERICAN BALLET THEATER
  Ethan Stiefel
  Adrienne Shulte
  Grant DeLong
PHILDANCO
  Devin Roberts
NORTH CAROLINA DANCE THEATER
  Annie Gerberich
BALLET AUSTIN I
  Chris Butler
  Lauren Bettencourt
BOSTON BALLET II
  Nadia Vostrikov
RICHMOND BALLET
  Lynne Bellinger

Index

Adra Hopper School, 23
Alabama Ballet, 67-72, 91, 104, 106, 108
Aldrich, 12, 90
Allwein, Katrina, 100
Alsedek, Anne, 100
Anacan, Antonio, 90
Arbaczewski, 90
Ashley Bouder, 84, 117
Ashley, Merill, 47
Atlanta Ballet, 30, 104
Atwood, 90
Avery, 90-91
Baker, 100
Balanchine Trust, 42-44, 48, 50, 59, 60, 83, 114
Balanchine, George, 1-2, 7-10, 12-13, 17-18, 24, 42-43, 47-48, 59, 67-69, 92, 103, 108, 113-114
Ballet Academy East, 48-49, 96, 107
Ballet Philippines, 105
Barnes, 91
Berdo, Laszlo, 94, 100
Bernstein, Leonard, 18
Beyond Technique, 12
Boston Ballet, 60, 83, 91, 100, 103-104, 117, 124
Brooklyn Academy of Music, 10
Capistrano, 46, 47, 50, 51
Carlisle Barracks, 54
Carlisle Project, 4, 11, 44, 82-83, 102, 112
Choreoplan, 86, 100, 104
Comeau, Maia, 101, 121
Cook, Richard, 2, 40, 43, 45, 60-61, 82, 94, 101, 109
Costume Society of America, 70, 108
CPYB, 1-2, 4-5, 10-11, 13, 18-19, 25-26, 32-33, 35, 38-39, 41-50, 55-56, 58-62, 70-72, 77-80, 83-88, 90-112, 114, 117, 124
Crawford, Theresa, 49, 93, 101
Dance Magazine, 69, 96, 114
Dance USA, 7, 12
Darhower, Marcia, 91, 98

de Ribere, Andre, 1-2, 14-16, 25, 32, 35, 39, 49, 82, 87, 121
de Ribere, Lisa, 10, 15, 17, 19, 25, 47, 58, 82, 83, 92, 98
DeAngelo, 92
Department of Defense, 62, 76
Dickinson College, 4-5, 29, 30, 32-33, 59, 78, 84-85, 88-89, 96, 127
Don Mowery, 79
Drosselmeyer, 14-15, 17-18, 58, 72, 82
Dubno, Julia, 48
Dunham Hospital, 55
Durden, William, 89, 127
Eppley, Sara, 102
Felixbrod, Trevor, 48
Fields, Ann, 102
Ford Foundation, 4, 10-11, 92, 112
Gershwin, George, 20
Gibson, Richard, 41
Gildea, 92
Gill, 49, 93
Gluck, Louise, 73
Good, Alecia, 102
Graham, Martha, 3
Greene, Haydee, 2, 93, 52, 57, 121
Greene, Kate, 56, 93
Greene, Robert, 53-54
Grigorian, Rafael, 12, 103
Hamburg Ballet, 44, 115, 117, 124
Hammerstein, Oscar, 57
Hargrave, Conn, 64
Havana, Cuba, 52
Heberlig, Wayne, 78
Hench, Leslie, 49, 75, 103
Hench, Tara, 49, 104, 117
Hench, Zachary, 49, 104
Hench, Zachery, 117
Hershey Theater, 15, 32, 43, 60, 72, 82, 83
Hineline, Alan, 2, 5, 39, 49, 62, 70, 72, 84-88, 104, 108, 125
Hirsch, 93
Hoffman, Robert, 17
Hoke, Simon, 93
Hoover, Darla, 2, 12, 26, 43-44, 46, 49, 60, 70, 84, 105, 121
Hsieh, 94

Imler, Carrie, 58-59, 62, 117
Imler, Nancie, 43-44, 49, 58, 61, 83, 121
Intrieri, Anita, 105
Jirard, 94
Joffrey Ballet, 44, 102, 106, 114
Jones, Maurinda, 49
Jones, Melinda, 49
Jung, Carl, 30
Jurgensen, Craig, 3, 5, 49, 94, 124, 127
Jurgensen, Heather, 44, 94, 115, 117
Jurgensen, Susan, 94
Kaiser, Roy, 12
Karinska, Barbara, 67, 69
Kinesiology for Dance, 29
Kirstein, Lincoln, 9
Kubanda, 94
Lavery, Sean, 47, 98, 100, 103, 113
Laws, Kenneth, 2, 5, 19, 28, 33, 35-36, 39, 49, 78, 87, 121
Laws, Priscilla, 29, 36
Lawyer, Shellie, 105
LeBlanc, Laurie, 94
LeBlanc, Sherri, 95
LeBlanc, Shirley, 105
LeBlanc, Tina, 43, 95, 114, 117
Life Magazine, 40
Linshes, Barbara, 8
Littlefield sisters, 9
Loughran, 95
Malina, Stuart, 127
Marcia Dale School of Dance, 1, 10, 17, 25, 29-30, 46, 55, 58-59, 70, 74-75, 77, 82, 92, 98, 101, 106, 113, 123
Marcia Dale Weary, 81
Marcia Dale Weary Endowment, 85
Maria von Trapp, 52
Marionette School of Dance, 9
Martins, Peter, 18, 47-48, 100, 113
Matluk, Bryan, 87-88
Mayra Worthen Ballet School, 64, 66, 68
McAvoy, 95
Middlebury College, 76
Miller, Ashley, 95
Moll, Karl, 96
Monroe, Josh, 106
Morales, Haydee, 43, 60
Mother Ginger, 34, 37-38, 50, 59, 72, 92
Nash, David, 11, 86-87, 106
National Endowment for the Arts, 7, 86
National Endowment of the Arts, 12
Neumeier, John, 115

New York City Ballet, 117
New York City Ballet Company, 10, 15, 17, 25, 26, 42, 47-48, 69, 88, 92, 109, 113, 115
New York Times, 70, 83, 85-86, 111, 124
Ninos, Karen, 106
Northeast Regional Ballet Festival, 11, 60
Nutcracker, 4, 14-15, 17, 19, 23, 31, 34, 37-39, 42-44, 47-48, 50, 59, 60, 62, 67-71, 82-83, 85-86, 90-99, 101-103, 106, 108-110, 113, 114
Only One Dream at a Time, 23
Pacific Northwest Ballet, 30, 59, 62, 90, 94, 117, 124
Paris Opera Ballet, 16
Parkinson syndrome, 34
Peabody Preparatory Institute, 12
Pennsylvania Ballet, 7, 10-12, 17, 23, 41, 50, 87, 91, 92, 95, 98, 102-104, 111, 113, 117, 124
Pennsylvania Council on the Arts, 43, 60, 84, 88, 127
Pennsylvania State University, 9, 12
Philadelphia Inquirer, 29
Physics and the Art of Dance, 30
Purchase College of the State University of New York, 44
Rabassi-Davis, AnnaMarie, 106
Reed, Jason, 86, 107
Reeder, Brian, 96
Rendell, Edward, 26, 115
Rene, Leon, 46, 51
Riseling, Jonathan, 48, 107
Robbins, Jerome, 18, 48, 113
Robert Gregor, 2, 37
Rockwell, Norman, 40
Rodgers, Richard, 57
Romeo, Simone, 96
Roosevelt, Theodore, 66
Royal Conservatory of Dance, 41
San Francisco Ballet, 26, 30, 44, 89, 95, 98-99, 104, 113-114, 124
SAN FRANCISCO BALLET, 117
San Francisco Ballet School, 26, 90
School of American Ballet, 7-9, 47, 48, 59, 88, 92, 96, 102-104, 109, 113, 115
Schulte, Bonnie, 88
Simon, Victoria, 43, 44
Skaggs, Sarah, 89
Smith, Betty, 2, 64, 67-72, 108, 121
Smith, Julia, 97

Snyder, Grace, 97
Sorrell, Patricia, 108
Sound of Music, 52, 57
Stafford, Abi, 85, 108, 109, 117
Stafford, Jonathan, 88, 109, 117
Stravinsky, Igor, 18
Strawberry Square, 86
Summer Program, 49, 78, 84, 92, 95, 102, 105-108, 110
Summers, Scott, 109
Swarthmore College, 12
Sweigart, Matthew, 97
Teddy Bear, 64, 66
Temple University, 12
United States Institute for Theatre Technology, 67, 70, 108
Villella, 97, 110
Virginia Youth Ballet, 110
Vostrikov, Gennadi, 12, 108, 110
Vostrikov, Susan, 110
Walborn, Sarah, 98
Warehouse, 5, 33-34, 43, 45, 50, 57, 71-72, 78
Watts, Heather, 47
Weary, Dale, 20, 25, 32, 43, 75, 77, 80, 82
Weary, Marcia Dale, 1, 2, 3, 5, 10-12, 16-17, 20, 26, 30, 38, 39, 41-43, 46, 55, 61, 70, 73, 85-89, 93, 98, 101, 103-104, 108, 112, 114, 121, 123, 125, 127
Weary, Melva, 32, 70, 77, 82, 123
Weary, Rosemary, 20-22, 74, 75, 80, 123
Weary, Sandra, 123
Weary, Sandra, 32, 73, 77, 80, 121
Weisberger, Barbara, 1, 2, 7-9, 13-14, 24, 41, 44, 82, 87, 91, 98, 121
Whitaker Center for Science and the Arts, 19, 33, 85, 86, 112
Whitaker Center for the Arts and Science, 5, 59
Whitaker Theater, 13
Whitaker, Kelly, 111
Whitesel, Donna Gregor, 37, 59, 98
Wilkes-Barre Ballet Theater, 10
Wilmarth, Emma, 99
Wingard, Maurinda, 2, 4-5, 11, 39, 50, 56, 62, 70-71, 78, 83, 86-87, 112
Witmer, Linda, p. back cover
Wolfe, Amanda, 111
York Strand Capitol Theater, 87
Zahorian, Vanessa, 99, 117

Acknowledgements

I am profoundly thankful to all of the individuals whom I interviewed in the preparation of this book. In each case, we formed a trusting relationship that brought forth historical material, rich in detail and deep in sentiment. To Marcia Dale Weary, Barbara Weisberger, Andre de Ribere, Kenneth Laws, Bob Gregor, Sandy Weary, Nancie Imler, Betty Smith, Darla Hoover, and Haydee Greene I say thank you for the time, stories, photographs, emails, proof reads, and your criticisms. I thank you also for your approval and your praise once we finalized the documents which I pledge will honestly and faithfully represent you. Thanks to Sarah Kopac for her kind assistance in the office.

I would like to thank my loving wife, Joan, for her patience and understanding during a two year span of research and relative isolation. I'm sure it seemed to Joan that at times, with my focus on the computer and hands on the keyboard, that I was in some other world.

Sincere thank you goes to Barbara Houston, Library Cataloger at the Cumberland County Historical Society, for her professional assistance in proofreading and word processing. Barbara was my spell-checker, editor, dash-and-comma-fixer, semicolon-placer, adjective-advisor, sentence-shortener, participle-undangler, metaphor translator, and pun referee. Without Barb, my grade in freshman English at Rutgers University might have been placed on recall.

A special thank you goes to Maia Comeau, Director of Congressional Affairs of the German Marshall Fund, for her personal and professional assistance in the preparation as well as the launch and social networking of this book. Her dedication and fondness for Marcia and the Central Pennsylvania Youth Ballet made her collaborative involvement in the book a mission. Her lively support and connectivity will contribute significantly to its success.

A profound thank you also is heaped on Kevin Graham of Graham Design, whose book production mastery in design, layout, formatting, page-setting, proofing, editing, spelling, inserting, and attaching made my first venture into authorship the joy of a lifetime.

The Barn – inside and out
— Craig Jurgensen

Marcia Dale Weary, Obituary

Marcia Dale Weary
March 31, 1936 – March 4, 2019
Obituary

Marcia Dale Weary passed away at the age of 82 on March 4, 2019. Marcia was born on March 31, 1936, the middle daughter of Dale and Melva Weary. She was survived at the time by her sisters, Sandra Weary and Rosemary Lyn Weary. Marcia initially founded the Marcia Dale School of Dance in 1955, where she taught classes daily and developed a teaching curriculum that is now trademarked and renowned in the industry for turning out exceptional dancers. Her vision was to give every child the opportunity to have access to exceptional ballet training. In 1974, the Marcia Dale School of Dance became the Central Pennsylvania Youth Ballet, a nonprofit school and performance company. Today, Central Pennsylvania Youth Ballet is an internationally recognized school of classical ballet. Thousands of young people have passed through its acclaimed studios. Alumni have been professional dancers in the top ballet companies of the world, including American Ballet Theater, New York City Ballet, Boston Ballet, San Francisco Ballet, Pacific Northwest Ballet, Miami City Ballet, Pennsylvania Ballet, National Ballet Theater of Canada, Les Ballets de Monte Carlo, Paul Taylor's American Modern Dance, and Hamburg Ballet (Germany), to name a few. Marcia was hailed as one of the greatest ballet teachers of the time. She forged the path from a local dance school to a global institution. Her unequaled dedication to her school, her students, and its instructors, plus her unique teaching style, brought Central Pennsylvania Youth Ballet to the top of the dance field. In 1989, the New York Times wrote, "Weary is considered one of the country's foremost ballet teachers, having produced dancers well known in the ballet world." According to Dance Teacher Magazine, "Marcia has produced dancers who embody the whole package—with attention to detail, early technical development, plus a broad socialization into the arts." Marcia never wavered from her vision to provide rigorous dance training for serious students and to enhance the cultural climate of the Central Pennsylvania region through ballet performances. Marcia remained active in CPYB throughout her entire life, teaching more than 25 classes per week well into her 80s. Marcia once said, "At every possible opportunity, I hope to instill in children a love for the arts and for classical music. Along with that, I hope to help them develop self-confidence, generosity, and the ability to focus." There is no doubt that Marcia accomplished all of this and more in her life, dedicated to teaching and to dancing. Her legacy lives on in all of the lives she has touched and in the strong organization that is the Central Pennsylvania Youth Ballet. CPYB is well positioned to continue to inspire, educate, and impact the lives of its students, the community, and the world at large. *The Sentinel*, March 11, 2019, Carlisle, Pennsylvania.

Administrative Staff
(September, 2023)

CHIEF EXECUTIVE OFFICER
Nicholas Ade

DIRECTOR OF CHILDREN'S AND PRIMARY DIVISIONS & DIRECTOR OF CURRICULUM
Rose Taylor

DIRECTOR OF PRE-PROFESSIONAL DIVISION & RESIDENT CHOREOGRAPHER
Alan Hineline

MEN'S PROGRAM COORDINATOR
Frederick Rocas

DIRECTOR OF ADMISSIONS AND OPERATIONS
Brigette Plummer

SENIOR DEVELOPMENT MANAGER
Paige Ade

CONTENT MARKETING MANAGER
Catherine Rogers

DISCOVERDANCE COORDINATOR
Wayne Ellis

OPERATIONS COORDINATOR
Juan Agudelo

CUSTOMER SUPPORT REPRESENTATIVE
Melanie McGrath

CUSTOMER SUPPORT REPRESENTATIVE
Alexandra Perry

ARTISTIC LEADERSHIP
Founder, Marcia Dale Weary
Chief Executive Officer, Nicholas Ade

Central Pennsylvania Youth Ballet
5 N Orange Street
Suite 3
Carlisle, Pennsylvania 17013
Phone: 717-601-2840

Recognized as one of the foremost ballet teachers of our time, Marcia Dale Weary has earned a national reputation for excellence. For more than five decades, Marcia's vision and determination have nurtured an extraordinary school, a professional-quality company, and a roster of unforgettable young performers, many of whom have gone on to celebrated professional careers. Recipient of a prestigious Governor's Award for the Arts for Outstanding Arts Leadership & Service to Youth, she is a true Pennsylvania artistic treasure.

- Philip Horn, Executive Director, Pennsylvania Council on the Arts

TEMPO DI MARCIA offers a striking testimony of one highly creative person's achievement to prepare expertly young people for ballet. It deftly affirms that education in the best sense – even that which targets an activity so specific as ballet – represents equal portions of professional discipline and life lessons.

- William G. Durden, President off Dickinson College, Carlisle, Pennsylvania

Craig Jurgensen beautifully captures the people and the spirit of one of the mid-Atlantic's cultural gems. A truly enjoyable read. Bravo!

- Stuart Malina, Music Director, Harrisburg Symphony Orchestra, and TONY Award Winner (2003)

www.ingramcontent.com/pod-product-compliance
Lightning Source LLC
LaVergne TN
LVHW020422070526
838199LV00003B/247